Build Reading Fluency
in 10-Minutes a Day

100 Reproducible Leveled Passages
Reading Levels 8th - 12th Grades

TWO PENCILS AND BOOK

Second Edition ISBN: 979-8345964309

Table of Contents

Table of Contents

Research Based

Why Fluency?

To be considered "on level" in reading fluency, high school students should be able to read aloud an unrehearsed passage, (i.e., either narrative or expository, fiction or non-fiction that is 200 to 300 words in length) from a grade-level text, with at least 95% accuracy in word reading. As students read aloud, their reading should sound as effortless as if they were speaking (Hasbrouck & Glaser, 2012.) This does not come easily for some students, which is why fluency practice is so essential.

In order to be considered fluent readers, students in grades 9 through 12 should be able to correctly read 150 words per minute (Hasbrouck & Tindal, 2006). In 2006 and again in 2010, Hasbrouck and Hasbrouck and Tindal (respectively) put forth that "[i]t is sufficient for students to read unpracticed, grade-level text at the 50th percentile of oral reading fluency norms" and that "…teachers do not need to have students read faster because there is no evidence that reading faster than the 50th percentile increases comprehension." See chart below.

The best strategy for developing and improving reading fluency is to provide students with many opportunities to read the same passages orally several times. These exercises provide such opportunities. On each passage, there is space for reading fluency calculations. The best part is that the passages are quick and make it easy for students to read aloud repeatedly – and often – without taking up a lot of valuable classroom time. The activities are designed as Day 1, Day 2 and Day 3 or all for one day.

In an updated 2017 study, Hasbrouck & Tindal reported that "students scoring 10 or more words below the 50th percentile using the average score of two unpracticed readings from grade-level materials need a fluency-building program."

Research suggests that one of the easiest and most effective ways for high school teachers to address reading fluency is to implement quick timed fluency into their weekly schedules.

Each of the passages are designed to be read 2 to 3 times each. A timer is set for 1 minutes. When the time rings, listener puts an X on the last word left. Let students finish passage and then calculate CWPM. Successful students read the passage with correct phrasing and attention to punctuation. Targets:

Grade	Fall	Winter	Spring
9-10	120-170 cwpm	130-180	140-190
11-12	130-180	140-190	150-200+

If you are building fluency – read each passage three times over two days. If you are reinforcing fluency – read passage 2 times in one day.

If you are using this for intervention, begin each passage as a guided reading. This is an evidence-based strategy for improving reading fluency. The student is asked to read the same passage three to five times, receiving feedback each time from the instructor or peer reviewer. Since this program is peer-to-peer, feedback comes from peers. By providing feedback on accuracy, rate and expression, students can incorporate those changes into each subsequent reading, eventually reaching a point of fluency with that particular passage. They can then move on to more difficult assignments.

Repeated readings of text can also contribute to better comprehension, one of the cornerstones of reading throughout life. All schools, from elementary to college, can easily provide students with repeated readings as well as paired passages of the same theme or topic.

For those teachers who want to mix-up full-class fluency lessons, one option is fluency-oriented reading instruction (FORI). This evidence-based practice begins with a teacher reading a particular passage aloud while students follow along in silent reading. Then, students read the passage aloud numerous times throughout the week, including echo, choral and partner reading. They also practice the passage for 15-30 minutes daily. At the end of a week, students engage in discussion, writing an essay or performing other activities that prove comprehension of the passage.

For optimum practice – complete passages in Sets 1-4 in order. Once students complete the Sets 1-4, which are leveled and in order, move on to Set 5. Set 5 is a series of fluency passages that move between levels.

Option 2: Administer Fluency exam. Pair like level students are work through fluency passages at their level. This resource is easy to differentiate – as students are paired – and while each pair of students must have the same fluency passage – each set of pairs do not.

Varying levels from day- to-day mimics real life reading situations and allows for optimum fluency and comprehension. For this set, students read a passage in article form, complete a quick comprehension check and then move on to timed-fluency practice of the same article.

Why Lexile Measures and Fluency?

Lexiles help us measure the levels at which one reads fluently. Lexiles range from 200 for beginning readers to 1700 for advanced readers. Lexile text below 200 represents beginning-reading material, and a student's Lexile score may have a number in the 100s or the code of BR. BR is a code that stands for Beginning Reading. When reading at a students appropriate Lexile level, comprehension should be at least 75%.

What are the reading demands of the post-secondary world according to Lexile Measures?

Median Text Measures (Williamson, 2004):

11th/12th grade (LA/SS textbooks):	(1090L)
GED Test Materials:	(1060L)
SAT/ACT Test Materials:	(1180L)
Military (training/field manuals):	(1180L)
Citizenship (newspapers, voting, jury):	(1230L)
Workplace (Daggett study materials):	(1260L)
Postsecondary - first two yrs. (textbooks):	(1355L)
University	(1395L)
Community College	(1295L)

Entry-level Occupational Reading Materials - Career Clusters (Daggett, 2003):

Agriculture/Natural resources	(1270-1510)
Architecture/Construction	(1210-1340L)
Arts/AV Technology/Communications	(1100-1190L)
Business and Administration	(1210-1310L)
Education and Training	(1320-1370L)
Health Science	(1260-1300L)
Hospitality and Tourism	(1230-1260L)
Human Services	(1050-1200L)
Law and Public Safety	(1420-1740L)
Manufacturing	(1200-1310L)
Retail/Wholesale Sales and Service	(1180-1270L)
Scientific Research/Engineering	(1190-1250L)
Transportation, Distribution and Logistics	(1170-1350L)

Why do high school students need to practice fluency?

An examination of K–12 texts using Lexile levels reveals a gap of 65L to 230L between high school seniors and the difficulty of postsecondary texts. Texts required for postsecondary college and career fall within a Lexile range of 1200L to 1400L, while the text complexity of typical high school textbooks for grades 11 and 12 is about 1050L to 1165L.

This research provides valuable insight into the apparent disconnect when high school graduates encounter college and career texts. To put this gap in perspective, a 250L difference between reader ability and text complexity can cause a drop from 75-percent comprehension to 50-percent comprehension. This means that high school seniors who can successfully read twelfth-grade texts may enter college or the workplace several months later and encounter texts that result in less than 50-percent comprehension (Williamson, 2008).

Lexile Grade Level Reading Chart				
Grade	Far Below	Approaching Grade Level	Meets Grade Level	Exceeds Grade Level
1	111 L and Below	110L – 185L	190L-530L	535L and Above
2	150L and Below	115L-415L	420L-650L	655L and Above
3	265L and Below	270L-515L	520L-820L	825L and Above
4	385L and Below	390L-735L	740L-940L	945L and Above
5	500L and Below	505L-825L	830L-1010L	1015L and Above
6	555L and Below	560L-920L	925-1070L	1075L and Above
7	625L and Below	630L-965L	970L-1120L	1125L and Above
8	660L and Below	665L – 1005L	1010L – 1185L	1190L and Above
9	775L and Below	780L-1045L	1050L-1260L	1265L and Above
10	830L and Below	835L-1075L	1080L – 1335L	1340 and Above
11 and 12	950 L and Below	995L-1180L	1185-1385L	1390L and Above

This resources comes with standards-based comprehension questions to be used with each of the readings. If you would like sample answers for these questions for each of these passages – please email twopencilsandabook@gmail.com. Please type "HS Fluency 1" in the body of the email. Answers for each passage.

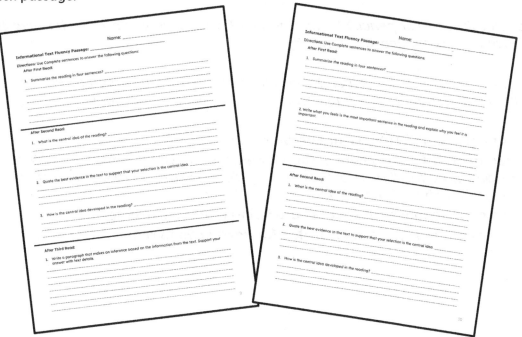

These passages are designed to check and increase fluency at the high school level.

Instructions and Script

Before you begin, have a copy of one passage for each student. The PDF can be displayed before the whole class on a Smartboard or printed and projected on a document camera. As you explain the lessons, demonstrate what students will be doing.

Explain what fluency is - the rate and ease at which we read along with the flow of reading. Review any names that may be different. Why? Some names do not follow English language rules or are foreign. They should not be counted as incorrect, nor should they cause students to pause.

About breaking students into pairs. If you are working with a group of students with varying abilities - pair like-leveled students together.

Explain the entire activity, as well as how to calculate combined words per minute, or CWPM. Then read the passage aloud. Have students track on their sheets as you read aloud. It is extremely beneficial for struggling students to hear the passage before they read it aloud. The goal isn't to have students stumble, but to optimize opportunities for ultimate success.

The first few times you do fluency as a class – the script below may be helpful:

1. **Check to make sure each person is in the right spot and then read the passage.**
2. **After you read the selected passage aloud, partner students and say something like:** *Put your name on your paper. Since you need to be marking your partner's paper, switch papers now. Raise your hand if you are Partner 1.*
3. **Pause until one student from each pair has their hand raised - acknowledge students when one person of each pair has their hand raised.**
4. **Raise your hand if you are Partner 2.** Pause until the other student from each pair has their hand raised – acknowledge students when the other partner has their hand raised.

    Excellent. When I say "Begin", all Partner 1s should quietly begin to read to their partners.

    All Partner 2s will use their pencils to keep track of their partner's errors. Partner 2s will put a line over each word pronounced incorrectly.

    When the timer goes off, all Partner 2s will circle the last word read, but Partner 1s will keep reading until the passage is complete. Does anyone have any questions?

5. Set the timer for one minute. If there are no questions - *Begin.*
6. When the timer goes off give chance for students to finish: *Partner 2s, please mark your partner's score and give feedback to Partner 1s. To calculate CWPM subtract the number of errors from the total number of words read.*
7. Walk around the room to make sure scores are being marked correctly.
8. Make sure students are ready and then switch for Partner 2s to read.

    Ready? Begin.

Name: _____

Fluency Passage: _____

Directions: Use Complete sentences to answer the following questions:

After First Read:

1. Summarize the reading in four sentences: _____

_____

_____

_____

_____

_____

_____

After Second Read:

1. What is the central idea of the reading? _____

_____

_____

_____

_____

2. Quote the best evidence in the text to support that your selection is the central idea. _____

_____

_____

_____

3. How is the central idea developed in the reading? _____

_____

_____

_____

After Third Read:

1. Write a paragraph that makes an inference based on the information from the text. Support your answer with text details.

_____

_____

_____

_____

_____

_____

_____

Name: _____

Text Fluency Passage: _____

Directions: Use Complete sentences to answer the following questions:

After First Read:

1. Summarize the reading in four sentences: _____
_____
_____
_____
_____
_____
_____

2. Write what you feels is the most important sentence in the reading and explain why you feel it is important.
_____
_____
_____
_____
_____
_____

After Second Read:

1. What is the central idea of the reading? _____
_____
_____
_____
_____

2. Quote the best evidence in the text to support that your selection is the central idea. _____
_____
_____
_____

3. How is the central idea developed in the reading? _____
_____
_____
_____

Set I: Practice Passages 6I0L-800L

Passage 1: The Machine Stops 1

Passage 2: The Machine Stops 2

Passage 3: The Machine Stops 3

Passage 4: The Machine Stops 4

Passage 5: The Machine Stops 5

Passage 6: The Machine Stops 6

Passage 7: The Machine Stops 7

Passage 8: The Machine Stops 8

Passage 9: The Machine Stops 9

Passage 10: The Machine Stops 10

Passage 11: The Machine Stops 11

Passage 1: The Machine Stops: Part 1

It was difficult for her to get used to at first. She missed the physical contact.	16
She missed the fresh air and the sun and the sand and the sky. She missed the	33
waves at the ocean and the breeze dancing off the snowy mountaintops. And	46
then she didn't.	49
It took a while to get used to life after the Machine, but it fell upon them so	67
gradually…one app at a time…one task at a time…so that after a while…the	84
Machine became synonymous with life and then life became something else	95
altogether.	96
After the virus and the takeover, the Machine was the only way to live in peace.	111
The earth beyond inhabitable, the machine saved them – the machine was the	122
answer of the ages – only she wondered – and then she didn't.	135
Imagine, if you can, a small room, hexagonal in shape like the cell of a single	151
bee in an enormous hive. Lit at either end, neither by window nor by lamp, yet	167
filled with a soft radiance. There were no openings for ventilation, but the air was	181
fresh. There were no musical instruments, and yet, a melody floated through the	194
air.	196
A recliner in the center, at its side a small desk. In the recliner sat a swaddled	213
figure - a young woman, about five feet eight, with a face as white as clouds – if	229
they still existed – and eyes a piercing blue. It was to her the little room belonged.	244
She was twenty-one, at last count. She remembered life before the Machine – only	257
less and less as one day turned to the next – colorful reminiscences fading into	270
desaturated monochromic memories – soon to be gone under the colorless	279
perpetual hum of the Machine – a giver sans red apple	293
A tone pierced the filtered silence.	299

Words Read: _____	Words Read: _____	Words Read: _____
minus mistakes: _____	minus mistakes: _____	minus mistakes: _____
equals cwpm: _____	equals cwpm: _____	equals cwpm: _____

Passage 2: The Machine Stops: Part 2

A tone pierced the filtered silence.	06
The young woman touched an invisible screen before her, and the room fell	19
silent.	20
"I guess I have to answer that," she thought begrudgingly, as she set her chair	34
in motion. The chair, like the music, was automated – controlled by a massive Wi-	46
Fi in the heart of the Machine. It moved her to the other side of the room where	64
the tone sounded loudly.	70
"Who is it?" she called. Her voice rife with an irritation disproportionate to the	84
interruption, only she had been interrupted often since the music began and she	97
just wanted to rest. She knew several thousand people. In some ways, human	110
interaction had advanced significantly. Sometimes there was too much mental	120
contact, too many apps, too much to do.	128
But when she listened to the voice emanating from thin air, her white face	142
blazed into smiles: "Wait! Wait! I'd love to talk. Lemme isolate myself. Nothing	155
important should happen for the next five minutes anyway. Then I have to deliver	168
my lecture on *Music during the Period Above*." Tempest was a chosen speaker –	181
granted with the gift to do *lives*. Not everyone earned that privilege, and she	194
guarded it cautiously.	199
Tempest touched the isolation app, so that no one else could speak to her. Then	213
she touched the lighting apparatus, and the little room plunged into darkness.	225
"Are you there?!" she called, her irritation returning. "Hailey?! Hello? Sitting here	237
in the dark wasting my time." She called to no response. She sighed. Tempest	252
picked up her device.	257

Words Read: _____	Words Read: _____	Words Read: _____
minus mistakes: _____	minus mistakes: _____	minus mistakes: _____
equals cwpm: _____	equals cwpm: _____	equals cwpm: _____

Passage 3: The Machine Stops: Part 3

It was a full fifteen seconds before the paper-thin tablet she now held in her hands	17
began to glow. She hated to pick it up. It was so personal. Hailey would be so close.	35
Dangling on the invisible screen in the air put a safe distance between them – only	50
Hailey's pod was so far away – sometimes the overhead wasn't powerful enough to	63
receive the signal these days.	68
A faint blue light irradiated her screen, it darkened to purple, and presently she could	83
see the image of one of her best friends from when they were above. From when they	100
walked the earth, but who now lived on the other side of the planet.	114
"You're so slow."	117
The other girl smiled nervously.	122
"You totally love annoying me," Tempest giggled. Seeing Hailey settled her into herself	134
– her old self – the person she used to be. She thought it annoying.	147
"I've called you a million times. You're always busy or isolated. I try to get your	163
attention on your lives, but you ignore my comments. I have something important to tell	178
you."	179
"If it is so important, why didn't you just text?" Tempest signed.	191
"Because this is something I have to say."	199
"Saying's overrated."	201
"I need you to come and see me."	209
Tempest watched her friend's face in the tablet, searching for a reason to justify the	224
extraneous emotion it displayed. Emotions rarely surfaced anymore. The Machine fixed	235
that - calmed them in the days after the war and the gradual isolation and	253
interdependence served to render emotion an obsolete irritant.	261
"I *can* see you!" she exclaimed. "You're right there."	270

Words Read: _____	Words Read: _____	Words Read: _____
minus mistakes: _____	minus mistakes: _____	minus mistakes: _____
equals cwpm: _____	equals cwpm: _____	equals cwpm: _____

Passage 4: The Machine Stops: Part 4

"I *can* see you!" she exclaimed. "You're right there." | 09

"I want to see you in person not through the flipping Machine," Hailey snapped. "I | 23
want to speak to you face-to-face." | 31

"It's overrated," Tempest said calmly, "and don't talk bad about the Machine." | 43

"Why not?" Hailey asked pointedly. | 48

"Because you can't." | 51

"Yes, I can. It's a machine, not the god you all portend it to be!" cried Hailey. "It isn't | 70
you know. A god? It's not even human. It was invented by humans. It's just the internet, | 87
on steroids, but the internet nonetheless." | 93

"It's different now." | 96

"Facebook, TikTok, the Machine, big brother. All the same." | 105

"I'll swipe you off if you don't stop." | 113

"One app too many, Uncle Steve." | 119

"Steve who?" Tempest snapped. She hated to be irritated. | 129

"Jobs, you dork. Steve Jobs." | 134

"Robert Kahn invented the internet." | 139

"Jobs changed how the world interacts and now we have this." | 150

"Stop talking about the founders with such insolence. Respect the Machine." | 161

"They are not the founding..." Hailey sighed, exasperated. "Man made the Machine | 173
and the apps that control our lives. Don't forget that. Great men maybe, but men either | 189
way. The Machine's a lot, but it's not everything." | 198

"It's everything I need. Everything anybody needs. I eat, I sleep, I have my hobbies - | 213
I even see my friends." | 218

"You don't see me anymore than I see you. I see something like you through this | 234
thing, but it isn't really you. I hear something like you through these speakers, but I | 250
don't hear you. Which brings me to why I need you to come and pay me a visit, so that | 270
we can meet face to face, and talk about the hopes and dreams we used to have. Talk | 288
about what's on my mind. It's been four years since the end of the insurrection wars. | 304
It's been longer since the vaccinated water eradicated the virus." | 314

Words Read: _____	Words Read: _____	Words Read: _____
minus mistakes: _____	minus mistakes: _____	minus mistakes: _____
equals cwpm: _____	equals cwpm: _____	equals cwpm: _____

Passage 5: The Machine Stops: Part 5

"It's been four years since the end of the insurrection wars. It's been longer	14
since the vaccinated water eradicated the virus," Hailey said.	23
Tempest replied that she could scarcely spare the time for a visit.	35
"That's such crap," Hailey huffed.	40
"It's not," Tempest defended. "My lives. I have my lives."	50
"Speaking through the screen to a bunch of comments. How boring. Besides,	62
you really can do your coveted lives anywhere."	70
"Not anymore. I upgraded. I'm totally immobile now. Completely synced in	81
my pod."	83
"Tragic," Hailey sighed. "What are you lecturing on today?"	92
"It is a discussion about rain for people too young to have experienced it."	106
"What if they can now?" Hailey asked.	113
"Don't be crazy. Everyone knows the damage done directly after the wars	125
ended all rain."	128
"Just come," Hailey said again.	133
"No time," Tempest retorted.	137
"The blaster barely takes a full day to rush between me and you."	150
"I hate blasters."	153
"Why?"	154
"I completely hate seeing the horrible brown earth, and the sea, and the stars	168
when its dark. I get no ideas in a blaster."	178
"I don't get them anywhere else anymore."	185
"What kind of ideas can the air give you?" Tempest paused for an instant. She	200
was sixteen when the wars ended, and the Machine saved humanity. Now at	213
twenty-one, she was an expert. Her time, everyone's time – over the years	226
between then and now – was dedicated to learning and reading and thinking	238
and interacting – under the direction of the Machine of course.	248

Words Read: _____	Words Read: _____	Words Read: _____
minus mistakes: _____	minus mistakes: _____	minus mistakes: _____
equals cwpm: _____	equals cwpm: _____	equals cwpm: _____

Passage 6: The Machine Stops: Part 6

"Did you know that there are four big stars that form an oblong, and three stars	16
close together in the middle of the oblong, and then hanging from these stars are three	32
other stars?"	34
"No, I didn't, and I hate the stars. But did they give you an idea? Interesting; tell	51
me."	52
"I had an idea that they were like a man."	61
"I don't understand."	64
"The four big stars are the man's shoulders and his knees. The three stars in the	70
middle are like the belts we used to wear, and the three stars hanging are like a sword."	88
"A sword?"	90
"Yes, a sword. Like people used to carry, to kill animals and other men. You don't	106
remember swords?" Hailey sighed. "Tempest, you have to come and see me." *Before it's*	120
too late, she added to herself.	126
"It's not a great idea, but it is certainly original. When did it come to you first?"	143
"What are you talking about?" Hailey asked frustrated.	151
"The idea. About the stars looking like men."	159
"That's not the point!" Hailey was getting frustrated, but this was too important to let	174
go.	175
Tempest thought her friend's face looked sad, but she could not be sure. The Machine	190
purposely distorted nuances of expression. It only gave a general idea of people - an	204
idea that was good enough for all practical purposes. The imponderable bloom,	216
declared by a discredited philosophy to be the actual essence of feeling and human	230
contact, was rightly ignored by the Machine, just as the imponderable bloom of the	244
grape was ignored by the manufacturers of artificial fruit. Something "good enough"	256
had long since been accepted by all those left alive – or so she thought.	270
"The truth is," her friend continued, "I want to see these stars again. I want to run on	288
cool grass. I want to feel the sun on my face, and not from the blaster, but from the	307
surface of the earth, like we used to. I want to visit the surface of the earth."	324
"Hailey!" Tempest snapped.	327
"I want to go home," Hailey said quietly – as if she feared the Machine might object.	343
Tempest just sat, taking it all in.	350

Words Read: _____	Words Read: _____	Words Read: _____
minus mistakes: _____	minus mistakes: _____	minus mistakes: _____
equals cwpm: _____	equals cwpm: _____	equals cwpm: _____

Passage 7: The Machine Stops: Part 7

"Please, just come Tempest," Hailey almost begged. "If only to explain to me what the harm   16

of visiting the surface of the earth would be."   25

"No harm," Tempest replied, controlling herself. "But no advantage either. The surface of the   39

earth is only dust and mud, no life remains on it, and you'd need a respirator, or the outer air will   60

kill you. People die immediately in the outer air."   69

"So, they say. Whatever. I'll take a respirator and wear the suit."   81

Tempest carefully considered her words. Hailey could be unpredictable, or she used to be   95

anyway. The fun they had as girls. That seemed so long ago. A lifetime for them, before the wars,   114

before the destruction, before the isolation. Tempest hoped she could dissuade her friend from   128

such a dangerous expedition.   132

"It is contrary to the spirit of the age," Tempest asserted.   143

"What does that even mean?" Hailey sighed frustrated at how difficult her friend had   157

become. "Talk like Tempest. Not like some Machine Zombie."   166

"Take it back," Tempest said calmly. "They could be listening. Don't be contrary."   179

"Do you mean contrary to the Machine?" Hailey ignored her friend.   190

"Sort of…"   192

"Tempest, remember when you wanted to be dauntless…"   200

"That was just a book," Tempest said matter-of-factly.   210

"You raged during the wars and when the raids came, you fought for our families, and we   227

made night raids for food and water, and we were only thirteen – fourteen at the most. We, you   245

and me together, kept half of San Pedro alive – and half of San Pedro, and Gracie, sane."   262

"Keeping Gracie sane was probably the hardest thing about the wars," Tempest tried to   276

suppress the smile her memory evoked. "Besides, there's peace now and we don't have to think   292

about any of that anymore."   297

Hailey's image faded.   300

"Hailey? Hailey?"   302

But Tempest's call went unanswered. Hailey's either isolated herself or they'd been heard and   316

cut off.   318

For a moment Tempest felt lonely.   324

Then she generated the light, and the sight of her room, flooded with radiance and studded   340

with comforting apps for all her pleasures, revived her. There were app holograms floating   354

everywhere - swipes to call for food, for music, for clothing, even for some of the old television   371

shows she used to enjoy.   376

Words Read: _____	Words Read: _____	Words Read: _____
minus mistakes: _____	minus mistakes: _____	minus mistakes: _____
equals cwpm: _____	equals cwpm: _____	equals cwpm: _____

Passage 8: The Machine Stops: Part 8

There was the hot-bath app, which caused a basin of imitation marble to rise out of	17
the floor, filled to the brim with a warm deodorized liquid, water-like, but different.	32
There was the cold-bath swipe. There was the swipe that produced literature. And	46
there were of course the swipes by which she communicated with her friends. The room,	61
though it contained nothing, was in touch with all that she cared for in the world.	77
Tempest's next move was to turn off the isolation app, and all the accumulations of	92
the last three minutes burst through to her. The room filled with the noise of text tones,	109
and voice messages. What was the new food like? Could she recommend it? Has she	123
had any ideas lately? Did she have time to listen to the ideas of another? Would she	140
make an engagement to visit the public nurseries at an early date? Sometime this week	155
or month perhaps.	158
To most of these questions she replied with irritation - a growing reaction lately.	171
Tempest held an important position but lived like everyone else. Her adaptability to the	186
Machine elevated her to the level of elder. Others sought her opinion, and she gladly	201
gave it.	203
Today she said the new food was horrible. That she could not visit the public	218
nurseries because she was way too busy. That she had no ideas of her own but had just	236
been told one about seven stars shaped like a man: she doubted there was much to it.	253
Then she switched off her texts and conversations. It was time to deliver her live on	269
music. The clumsy system of public gatherings had been long since abandoned; neither	282
Tempest nor her audience needed to leave their rooms. Seated in her recliner she	296
spoke, while they, in their recliners heard, fairly well, and saw her hologram, fairly well,	311
and commented all too readily.	316
Tempest opened with a funny story and settled into an amusing talk of days gone by.	332
Her live, which lasted ten minutes, was well received, and at its conclusion she and	347
many of her audience listened to another's live on the sea; there were ideas to be had	364
from the sea; the influencer was the last person on earth to visit it. Tempest	379
remembered the sea, but she could no longer remember what the salty waves felt like.	314
She could no longer feel the wind in her hair. The sea was black now – daunting. Her	331
news app told her so.	336

Words Read: _____	Words Read: _____	Words Read: _____
minus mistakes: _____	minus mistakes: _____	minus mistakes: _____
equals cwpm: _____	equals cwpm: _____	equals cwpm: _____

Passage 9: The Machine Stops: Part 9

After the live she fed, talked to friends, had a bath, talked again, and	14
summoned her bed. She didn't like her bed. It was too big and too hard. Tempest	30
liked small beds. The one thing she remembered, the one thing she missed…was	44
her old bed and maybe touching…and of course her aunt…her loving, crazy aunt	59
who would not adapt to the Machine. Tempest briefly wondered what became of	72
her, but quickly put those thoughts aside. They were painful and unproductive.	84
She tried to get comfortable. Complaint was useless, for beds were of the	97
same dimension all over the world, and to have had an alternative size would	111
have involved alterations in the Machine. Tempest isolated herself, it was	122
necessary, for neither day nor night existed under the ground.	132
In isolation, she reviewed all that had happened since she'd summoned the	144
bed last. Ideas? Scarcely any. Events? Was Hailey's invitation an event? And	156
what did her friend really want? Tempest's days of trouble – the world's days of	170
trouble for that matter – were all behind them and all that trouble was from the	185
world above ground. Why would she even dream of going back up?	197
By her side, on the little desk, was a survival from the ages of litter - one	213
book. This was the Book of the Machine. In it were instructions against every	227
possible contingency. If she was hot or cold or at a loss for a word, she went to	245
the book, and it told her which app to summon. The Central Committee	258
published the Book of the Machine. It was richly bound – a remanent of the past	273
to emphasize its importance.	277
Sitting up in the bed, she took it reverently in her hands. She glanced round	292
the glowing room as if someone might be watching her. Then, half ashamed, half	306
joyful, she murmured "O Machine! O Machine!" and raised the volume to her lips.	320
Thrice she kissed it, thrice inclined her head, thrice she felt the delirium of	334
acquiescence. Her ritual performed, she turned to page 1367, which gave the	346
times of the departure of the blasters from ground in the northern hemisphere,	359
under whose soil she lived, to the island in the southern hemisphere, under which	373
her old buddy Hailey lived.	378

Words Read: _____	Words Read: _____	Words Read: _____
minus mistakes: _____	minus mistakes: _____	minus mistakes: _____
equals cwpm: _____	equals cwpm: _____	equals cwpm: _____

Passage 10: The Machine Stops: Part 10

She thought, "This is ridiculous."	05
She made the room dark and slept; when she woke, she made the room light;	20
she ate and exchanged ideas with her friends and listened to music and	33
watched an old television show and attended lives; she made the room dark and	47
slept. Above her, beneath her, and around her, the Machine hummed eternally;	59
she did not notice the noise, for she had been born with it in her ears. The earth,	77
carrying her, hummed as it sped through silence, turning her now to the invisible	91
sun, now to the invisible stars. She woke and made the room light again and	106
again.	107
And then it hit her. It had already happened.	116
Tempest summoned an app.	120
"Hailey."	121
"I won't talk to you," Hailey answered, "until you come."	131
"You already went. To the surface? You've already been to the surface."	143
The image faded.	145
Again, Tempest consulted the book. She laid back nervously in her chair.	157
Think of Tempest, so pale from lack of sun – skin was almost translucent.	170
Presently she directed the chair to the wall, and pressed an unfamiliar app. The	184
wall swung apart slowly. Through the opening a tunnel curved slightly, so that its	198
end was not visible. Should she go to see her friend, here was the beginning of	214
the journey.	216
Of course, she knew all about the communication-system. There was nothing	228
mysterious in it. She would summon a car, and it would fly with her down the	243
tunnel until it reached the lift that communicated with the blaster station. The	234
system had been in use for many years, long before the universal establishment	256
of the Machine. And of course, she'd studied the civilization into which she was	270
born. The civilization that no longer existed. The civilization that had mistaken	282
the functions of the system, and had used it for bringing people to things,	296
instead of things to people.	301

Words Read: _____	Words Read: _____	Words Read: _____
minus mistakes: _____	minus mistakes: _____	minus mistakes: _____
equals cwpm: _____	equals cwpm: _____	equals cwpm: _____

Passage 11: The Machine Stops: Part 11

Those funny old days, when men went for change of air instead of changing | 14
the air in their rooms! The days when people gathered in restaurants or | 27
purchased clothes in stores. And yet-she was frightened of the tunnel: she had | 41
not seen it since she visited her brother three years ago. It curved-but not quite | 57
as she remembered; it was brilliant-but not quite as brilliant as an influencer had | 72
suggested. Tempest was seized with the terrors of direct experience. She shrank | 84
back into the room, and the wall closed up again. | 94

"Hailey," she said, "I can't come to see you. I'm not well." | 106

Immediately an enormous apparatus fell out of the ceiling and surrounded | 117
her. A thermometer was automatically laid upon her heart. She sat powerless. | 129
Cool pads soothed her forehead. The Machine knew her every thought. | 140

Tempest spoke again. "You have been to the surface, haven't you? Something | 152
happened, didn't it?" | 155

"Not yet." | 157

"Then I don't get it." | 162

"I won't tell you through the machine." | 169

Tempest resigned to the Machine and was content with her life, but she was | 183
intelligent – intelligent enough to know the Machine heard and saw everything. | 194

Her mind wandered to Hailey and elementary school, through the insurrection | 205
and the wars and the virus, and then the isolation when the Machine assigned | 219
them rooms on opposite sides of the earth – as if being together was dangerous. | 233
There was something special about Hailey. | 239

'*There had been something special about me too*,' she thought. | 249

Tempest knew she had to go. She felt it. Again, she swiped the unfamiliar app, | 265
again the wall swung back. There was the tunnel that curved out of sight. | 278
Clasping the Book, she rose, tottered on to the platform, and summoned the car. | 292
Her room closed behind her; the journey to the southern hemisphere began. | 304

Words Read: _____	Words Read: _____	Words Read: _____
minus mistakes: _____	minus mistakes: _____	minus mistakes: _____
equals cwpm: _____	equals cwpm: _____	equals cwpm: _____

Set 2: 8th Grade Reading Level Passages - 810L-1000L

Name: _____

Passage 12: Serena Williams

Serena Williams is one of the greatest athletes of all time. She was once   14
ranked singles world No. 1 by the Women's Tennis Association for 319 weeks,   27
including a joint-record 186 consecutive weeks. She finished as the year-end No.   41
1 singles player five times. She has won 23 Grand Slam singles titles, the most by   57
any player in the Open Era, and the second-most of all time (behind Margaret   72
Court's 24 titles).   75

Serena has 39 Grand Slam titles. She holds titles in singles doubles and mixed   89
doubles. She is the only recent female player to hold four Grand Slam singles   103
titles at the same time. From the 2002 French Open to the 2003 Australian Open,   118
she was dominant, winning all four major singles titles (each time over her sister   132
Venus in the final) to achieve a non-calendar year Grand Slam and her career   147
Grand Slam, known as the "Serena Slam."   154

Serena's ranked as one of the highest paid athletes in the world. This doesn't   168
usually happen for woman. In 2019, she was ranked as the 63rd highest paid   182
athlete out of every athlete in the world. She's been on the Forbes' list of the 100 199
highest paid athletes more than once – most recently in 2021 when she was   212
ranked 28th of all men and women.   219

She's been commissioned to represent many brands over the course of her   231
career. She's represented Wilson, Gatorade, Delta Air Lines, IBM, Pepsi, Beats by   243
Dre, JP Morgan Chase, Audemars Piguet, Bumble, Upper Deck and Intel. She is   256
also the car brand Aston Martin's Chief Sporting Officer.   265

Serena's parents supported their daughter early in her career. They also   276
supported Serena's tennis playing sister: Venus. Their parents, however, made   286
the girls wait until they were 16 to enter the professional tennis world. The rest is 302
history.   303

Fun fact: Serena and her sister Venus are minority owners in the Miami   316
Dolphins Football team.   319

Words Read: _____	Words Read: _____	Words Read: _____
minus mistakes: _____	minus mistakes: _____	minus mistakes: _____
equals cwpm: _____	equals cwpm: _____	equals cwpm: _____

Passage 13: Sommer Ray

Sommer Ray is a social media influencer born on September 15, 1996. She has | 14
26 million Instagram followers - which makes her one of the platforms biggest | 26
influencers. She is a fitness model with her own YouTube channel where she | 39
vlogs with Amanda Cerny. Amanda is a fellow social media influencer. They are | 52
both on TikTok as well. | 57

Sommer moved from Colorado to Los Angeles in 2013. In 2017, she joined a | 71
group of YouTubers called the CloutGang squad. "CloutGang" features | 80
founder, FaZe Banks , FaZe Rug, Alissa Violet, Amar Koomz, Ugly God, | 91
and RiceGum. The web group was formed in response to Jake Paul and his | 105
former primarily online video blog and music group called "Team 10." | 116

Sommer is beautiful, but she is also exceptionally intelligent. She's been | 127
quoted saying being smart is more important than being beautiful. Sommer | 138
works hard and is focused on her fitness goals. She uses her fitness videos to | 153
grow a following. "People who want to gain a following but do nothing – can't. It | 168
just doesn't happen in the real world." | 175

Sommer started working on her dream as a young teen. She started | 187
modeling when she was only 14-years-old. When she turned 16, she became a | 202
fitness bikini model. In 2015, she won 1st place in the NPC Colorado State | 216
Championship for Teen Bikini. | 220

Sommer is quoted as saying: "…being attractive helps, but if fitness wasn't my | 233
career, no one would follow me." Think about it. Attaining the status of social | 247
influencer is only possible if you do something other than want to be a famous | 262
social media star. But her following is lucrative. She recently scooped up a 5- | 276
bedroom, 1.4-million-dollar house in L.A.'s San Fernando Valley. It seems all that | 290
intelligence and hard work has paid off. | 297

Words Read: _____	Words Read: _____	Words Read: _____
minus mistakes: _____	minus mistakes: _____	minus mistakes: _____
equals cwpm: _____	equals cwpm: _____	equals cwpm: _____

Passage 14: Excerpt from Tom Sawyer Chapter 1

The old lady pulled her glasses down and looked over them about the room;	14
then she put them up and looked out under them. She seldom or never	28
looked *through* them for so small a thing as a boy; they were her state pair, the	45
pride of her heart, and were built for "style," not service—she could have seen	60
through a pair of stove-lids just as well. She looked perplexed for a moment, and	76
then said, not fiercely, but still loud enough for the furniture to hear:	89
"Well, I lay if I get hold of round and I'll—"	99
She did not finish, for by this time she was bending down and punching under	114
the bed with the broom, and so she needed breath to punctuate the punches	128
with. She resurrected nothing but the cat.	135
"I never did see the beat of that boy!"	144
She went to the open door and stood in it and looked out among the tomato	160
vines and "jimpson" weeds that constituted the garden. No Tom. So she lifted up	174
her voice at an angle calculated for distance and shouted:	184
"Y-o-u-u TOM!"	188
There was a slight noise behind her and she turned just in time to seize a small	203
boy by the slack of his roundabout and arrest his flight.	214
"There! I might 'a' thought of that closet. What you been doing in there?"	228
"Nothing."	229
"Nothing! Look at your hands. And look at your mouth. What *is* that there?"	243
"I don't know, aunt."	247
"Well, I know. It's jam—that's what it is. Forty times I've said if you didn't let	264
that jam alone I'd skin you. Hand me that switch."	274
The switch hovered in the air—the peril was desperate—	284
"My! Look behind you, aunt!"	289
The old lady whirled round, and snatched her skirts out of danger. The lad fled	314
on the instant, scrambled up the high board-fence, and disappeared over it.	327

Words Read: _____	Words Read: _____	Words Read: _____
minus mistakes: _____	minus mistakes: _____	minus mistakes: _____
equals cwpm: _____	equals cwpm: _____	equals cwpm: _____

Passage 15: Excerpt from Bram Stoker's Dracula

4 May.—I found that my landlord had got a letter from the Count, directing	15
him to secure the best place on the coach for me; but on making inquiries as to	32
details he seemed somewhat reticent, and pretended that he could not	43
understand my German. This could not be true, because up to then he had	57
understood it perfectly; at least, he answered my questions exactly as if he did.	71
He and his wife, the old lady who had received me, looked at each other in a	88
frightened sort of way. He mumbled out that the money had been sent in a	103
letter, and that was all he knew.	110
When I asked him if he knew Count Dracula, and could tell me anything of his	126
castle, both he and his wife crossed themselves, and, saying that they knew	139
nothing at all, simply refused to speak further. It was so near the time of	154
starting that I had no time to ask anyone else, for it was all very mysterious and	171
not by any means comforting.	176
Just before I was leaving, the old lady came up to my room and said in a very	194
hysterical way:	196
"Must you go? Oh! young Herr, must you go?" She was in such an excited	211
state that she seemed to have lost her grip of what German she knew and mixed	227
it all up with some other language which I did not know at all. I was just able to	246
follow her by asking many questions. When I told her that I must go at once,	262
and that I was engaged on important business, she asked again:	273
"Do you know what day it is?" I answered that it was the fourth of May. She	290
shook her head as she said again:	297
"Oh, yes! I know that! I know that, but do you know what day it is?" On my	215
saying that I did not understand, she went on.	224

Words Read: _____	Words Read: _____	Words Read: _____
minus mistakes: _____	minus mistakes: _____	minus mistakes: _____
equals cwpm: _____	equals cwpm: _____	equals cwpm: _____

Passage 16: Richard Nixon

Richard Nixon was the 37th President of the United States. He served from	13
1969 until his resignation in 1974 after previously working as a U.S.	25
Representative and a U.S. Senator from California. After successfully ending	35
American fighting in Vietnam and improving international relations with the	45
U.S.S.R. and China, he became the only President ever to resign the office. His	59
resignation was the result of the Watergate scandal.	67
Nixon's time in office was accomplished. He ended the military draft, he	74
fostered anticrime laws, he implemented necessary environmental programs,	75
and he ended the bitter Vietnam War.	82
Even more notable, his push for world stability was astounding. He reduced	94
tensons with China and then the U.S.S.R. He worked with the Russian leader	107
Leonid Brezhnev and produced a treaty to limit nuclear weapons.	117
Nixon was an extremely popular president. In 1972, he won a second term as	131
president by the widest margin in history, then his world exploded.	142
Within months of this second election, his administration became besieged	152
with the Watergate scandal. Nixon was a republican. During the 1972 campaign,	164
there was a break-in at the offices of the Democratic National Committee.	177
The break-in was traced to the Committee to Re-elect the President. Nixon	191
denied he knew about it. He denied any involvement, then the Supreme Court	204
forced him to surrender tape recordings which showed he obstructed justice,	215
lied, and was involved. Not only was he involved, but he covered up his	229
involvement.	230
With impeachment looming, Nixon resigned. That was on August 9, 1974.	241
Nixon's crimes were pardoned by President Ford. Nixon spent his later life	253
writing books and speaking about foreign policy.	260

Words Read: _____	Words Read: _____	Words Read: _____
minus mistakes: _____	minus mistakes: _____	minus mistakes: _____
equals cwpm: _____	equals cwpm: _____	equals cwpm: _____

Name: _____

Passage 17: The Grand Canyon

The Grand Canyon is a mile-deep gorge in northern Arizona, northwest of | 13
Flagstaff. The canyon is over 270 miles long, up to 18 miles wide and a mile | 29
deep. This makes it one of the longest canyons in the world. Scientists estimate | 43
the canyon formed 5 to 6 million years ago when the Colorado River began | 57
carving through layers and layers of rock. | 64

The Grand Canyon contains some of the oldest exposed rock on Earth. The | 77
mammoth walls reveal a cross section of the Earth's crust going back almost | 90
two billions years. These layers continue to give geologist the opportunity to | 112
study evolution through time. The oldest rocks in the Grand Canyon are believed | 125
to be the Vishnu Basement Rocks found near the bottom of the Inner Gorge. | 139
They formed approximately 1.7 billion years ago. | 146

Artifacts have been discovered from humans that date back almost 12,000 | 157
years. Human occupation from the last ice age is evident. Fast forward to 1903 | 171
when President Teddy Roosevelt traveled to the Canyon and declared portions | 182
of the Canyon a federal game reserve. The Grand Canyon became a National | 194
Park in 1919 – just three years after President Woodrow Wilson created the | 206
National Park Service. | 209

Today, Grand Canyon National Park receives five million visitors per year. | 220
That's a far measure more than the 44,000 people who traveled to the park in | 235
1919. Much of the park remains the same as it has been for centuries. A recent | 251
addition is the Grand Canyon skywalk. The skywalk is a glass floor bridge that | 265
hangs over a section of the canyon. This bridge is not without controversy. Some | 279
say the bridge disturbs sacred grounds and is a blemish on sacred native lands. | 293
The bridge is owned by the Hualapai Tribe. The grand canyon is a natural | 307
wonder and a revered treasure for all to behold. | 216

Words Read: _____
minus mistakes: _____
equals cwpm: _____

Words Read: _____
minus mistakes: _____
equals cwpm: _____

Words Read: _____
minus mistakes: _____
equals cwpm: _____

29

Name: _____

Passage 18: Historical Figures: Who's More Significant?

Who was more significant: Washington or Lincoln? Hitler or Einstein? Jane | 11
Austin or William Shakespeare. That depends on who you ask and how you look | 25
at it. | 27

Significance is not about achievements. It's related to fame, but on a | 39
different metrics. Time Magazine, you know the publication that releases the | 50
annual "Person of the Year" - they did an extensive study using several data | 63
sources. They created an algorithm scanning things like Google search rankings, | 74
Wikipedia, millions of books and media references and made a list. They also | 87
adjusted for how today's stars, most of them anyway, will fade from cultural | 100
memory, but truly influential and significant people will not. | 109

Think about Justin Bieber. Ask most people worldwide and they've probably | 120
heard of him, but what about Chester A. Arthur. Does Chester ring any bells? | 134
Nope? He was the 21st president of the United States. Justin ranked 8,633 on | 148
Time's list. Chester ranked 499th. Why? Chester A. Arthur's reputation and | 159
significance is more stable. It will last over time. | 168

So, who are the most significant people in history, according to this algorithm | 181
anyway? Topping the list, in order, are Jesus, Napoleon, Muhammad, William | 192
Shakespeare, Abe Lincoln, George Washington, Adolph Hitler, Aristotle, | 200
Alexander the Great, and Thomas Jefferson. Those are the top ten. Women don't | 213
make the list until 13 and 16 – Elizabeth I of England and Queen Victoria – | 227
respectively. | 229

Of course, these rankings change. People go up and down, and if you are only | 244
looking at the top 100 – some are bound to be replaced. Think about Vladimir | 258
Zelensky? He's bound to have significant status that far exceeds many who are | 271
currently on the list. | 275

What do you think? Who would you rank as having significant staying power? | 288
Interesting to think about, isn't it? | 294

Words Read: _____	Words Read: _____	Words Read: _____
minus mistakes: _____	minus mistakes: _____	minus mistakes: _____
equals cwpm: _____	equals cwpm: _____	equals cwpm: _____

Passage 19: Iron Man

Iron Man is a comic book character published by Marvel and created by	13
comic super creator Stan Lee. Iron Man first appeared in print in 1963. This first	28
appearance was in *Tales of Suspense.* In May of 1968, Iron Man received his	42
own comic book debut - *Iron Man* #1. Also notable for Iron Man in 1963 was that	58
the character co-founded the Avengers alongside Thor, Ant-Man, Wasp and	70
the Hulk.	72
Iron Man's human name is Anthony Edward Stark. "Tony" is a wealthy	84
business magnate, philanthropist, inventor, and scientific genius. One day, Tony	94
is kidnapped. He sufferers a chest injury. When his captors attempt to force him	108
to build a weapon of mass destruction, he instead creates a mechanized suit of	122
armor to save his life and escape captivity. Later, Tony embellishes his suit,	135
adding weapons and other technological devices he designed through his	145
company, Stark Industries. He uses the suit to protect the world as Iron Man. At	160
first, he hides his true identity but eventually publicly reveals himself as Iron	173
Man.	174
Iron Man uses this suit to help protect the world. He advances his suit –	188
rebuilding it many times. His superpowers are based on technology rather than	200
physical ability.	202
Since creating his first suit, Iron Man has gone through numerous events	214
significant to his life. Originally, to cover for Tony Stark's escapades as Iron	227
Man, he convinced the world that Iron Man was his bodyguard. This helped	240
explain the perceived close ties between Stark and Iron Man to both the outside	254
world and even those who fought alongside Iron Man.	263
Did you know that Iron Man is a second-tier superhero? He is popular with	278
readers. He is an Avenger. But in the Marvel Universe, he is a secondary	292
character, or at least he was. That said – we love Iron Man.	314

Words Read: _____	Words Read: _____	Words Read: _____
minus mistakes: _____	minus mistakes: _____	minus mistakes: _____
equals cwpm: _____	equals cwpm: _____	equals cwpm: _____

Passage 20: Queen Elizabeth I (b. 1533, r. 1558 d. 1603)

Elizabeth I is one, if not thee, greatest monarch ever to reign over England.	14
Her military defeated the Spanish Armada in 1588 and saved England from	26
invasion. She established Protestantism in England, she secured and maintained	36
peace among her often unruly subjects and created an environment where arts	47
flourished and were revered.	52
Elizabeth I's reign is often called the English Renaissance. Her court became a	65
gathering place for writers, poets, musicians, and scholars. Her reign has also	77
been labeled the Elizabethan or "Golden Age" because it was a period of	90
tremendous advancement and achievement in England.	96
Elizabeth I made excellent use of both Parliament and the Privy Council. The	109
Privy Council is an advisory council of important officials. Elizabeth I was also	122
extraordinarily intelligent. Through most of her reign – most especially in her	133
first years as Queen, Elizabeth posed and lived rather dangerously in order to	146
survive. Her enemies, France and Spain, were richer, stronger and had more	158
global and regional influence than England. Elizabeth knew she would never	169
survive a direct attack from either. Instead, the queen played one against the	182
other – relying on smokescreens and confusion. She exploited France and	192
Spain's hostility towards each other. Hinting at aid to one and then the other.	206
She kept both guessing. She played the hero in the middle.	217
When Elizabeth I died in 1603, England was powerful and expanding. It had	229
grown a rich trade in the Netherlands, the Mediterranean, the Middle East and	242
Russia. She constructed the base for the first English settlement in the New	255
World - established in Virginia only four years after her death.	265
Queen Elizabeth I set the foundation for one of the strongest empires of the	279
modern era. She truly is one of England's most successful rulers.	311

Words Read: _____	Words Read: _____	Words Read: _____
minus mistakes: _____	minus mistakes: _____	minus mistakes: _____
equals cwpm: _____	equals cwpm: _____	equals cwpm: _____

Passage 21: At Dinner

"First and ten, do it again, we like it, we like it." Mom cheered as she passed	17
the tacos.	19
"I have no idea what that even means?" Hailey rolled her eyes at her mother.	34
"It's a cheer," Mom said brightly.	40
"Not anymore," Hailey took two tacos. Cheerleading practice made her	50
hungry and tacos were her favorite food.	57
"Actually, it still is," Hailey's twin sister Bailey replied stuffing her taco with	70
peppers and cheese. "Do you even know what it means?"	80
"Someone scores the first ten points, and someone wants them to do it	93
again?" Hailey guessed.	96
Dad almost choked on his taco and tried not to laugh. Bailey was not so nice.	112
"Um no."	114
"Then, if you're so smart, what does it mean? Never mind. I could care less. I	130
just have to say the words and do the skills. Oh, and be cute. I have to be cute.	149
I'm very good at that."	154
"It would help if you understood the cheers," Dad interjected.	164
"And how they relate to the game. Like you should know you wouldn't do that	179
cheer at a basketball game," Bailey advised.	186
"And why not?" Hailey asked her sister.	193
"Because it's a football cheer. A team gets four tries to move the ball ten	208
yards. If they make it – they keep the ball. If they don't – the other team gets it.	225
You're going to embarrass yourself."	230
"Wow, that sounds easy. You'd think people would score more points," Hailey	242
said. She finished her dinner, cleared the table, and went upstairs to study up on	257
football a bit. The last thing she wanted was to be embarrassed.	269

Words Read:	Words Read:	Words Read:
minus mistakes:	minus mistakes:	minus mistakes:
equals cwpm:	equals cwpm:	equals cwpm:

Passage 22: Peter Parker

Peter Parker played the piano. Peter Parker played the piano well. Peter	12
Parker played the piano daily. People came from miles around to hear Peter	25
Parker play.	27
Peter Parker was a high school senior. He went to school. He went to class. He	43
talked to his friends, and then he went home and played the piano. He played the	59
piano for three hours every day. After dinner, Peter Parker did his homework,	72
then he played for another hour before he went to bed.	83
Peter Parker wanted to be a professional piano player. He wanted to write	96
songs and play the piano. His mom encouraged him. Peter was very good. His	110
dad encouraged him. His grandmother paid for his piano lessons.	120
"Even great piano players need lessons," Grandmother said.	128
Peter happily agreed. His lessons were on Saturday.	136
One day, Peter got a letter in the mail. It was from the San Francisco	151
Symphony. They had a special youth program. Peter Parker's teacher submitted a	162
video on behalf of Peter. The letter said Peter could try out.	175
Peter was very excited. On the day of tryouts, he couldn't even eat. Peter took	189
BART to the tryouts. His mom or dad would have driven him, even Grandmother	203
offered to drive him, but Peter wanted to use the time to think.	217
Mom, Dad and Grandmother waited on pins and needles for Peter to get	230
home. Peter left home at 8 o'clock in the morning and did not spring back through	244
the door until six that evening. He was all smiles.	255
"I made it. I'm in!" Peter hugged his family. They all went out to celebrate.	270

Words Read:	Words Read:	Words Read:
minus mistakes:	minus mistakes:	minus mistakes:
equals cwpm:	equals cwpm:	equals cwpm:

Passage 23: Devon's Dogs

Devon had just turned seventeen and wanted to buy the bright blue Honda	13
Civic his cousin was selling. Devon made a deal with his father to help finance the	28
vehicle. If Devon got a job and raised $2000.00, his father would make up the	43
difference with a no interest loan.	50
The Civic was practically new but Tanner, Devon's cousin, was moving to	62
England for graduate school. He'd be there for two years and couldn't take the	76
car with him.	79
Jobs in Devon's area were difficult to come by, so Devon mapped out a plan.	94
He would start a dog walking business. Dad helped Devon make flyers and	107
passed them around the neighborhood. They got permission to put one up at their	120
local store, in the library, and on the community bulletin board. Then, they went	134
home and waited.	138
That evening, Devon got six texts, two calls, and set up appointments with	151
five people. Out of those five, all wanted Devon to walk their dogs.	164
In no time, Devon had more dog walking requests than he could	176
accommodate. It took him almost two months, but he finally had his portion of	190
the money.	192
Devon was walking dogs when Tanner brought the car over. When Devon saw	204
it in the driveway, he ran into the house and up the stairs to his room. He came	222
back down with a jar full of money. Dad wrote a check for the rest.	238
Tanner tossed him the keys with a big grin. "There you go little cousin. Take	253
care of her."	256
"Come on," Devon excitedly exclaimed, "let's go for a ride."	266
Devon loved the car. Tanner loved the hamburgers his uncle bought them	278
after they circled the neighborhood for a full hour before Devon could be	291
persuaded to stop driving and have a meal.	299

Words Read:	Words Read:	Words Read:
minus mistakes:	minus mistakes:	minus mistakes:
equals cwpm:	equals cwpm:	equals cwpm:

Name: _____

Passage 24: The Springs Mountains

The Spring Mountains are near Las Vegas, Nevada and named after the	12
number of water springs found there. The Spring Mountains divide two	23
watersheds that drain into the Colorado River watershed.	31
A watershed is a series of rivers and springs that drain into a common source.	45
The highest point on the Spring Mountains is Mount Charleston. The whole area is	57
a protected wilderness.	63
Spring Mountain is open year-round and offers hiking and camping. Day	75
visitors can picnic. Winter visitors play in the snow, ski, and snowshoe.	88
Technically, the Spring Mountains are in the desert however the natural springs	100
create a lush forest – an oasis in the barren desert.	110
The mountains vary in elevation with high peaks that roll down to lowland	123
valleys. The varying elevation creates many and diverse "life zones." Low	134
elevations support sagebrush and Joshua trees, middle elevation boast a	144
"Pinyon-Juniper" ecosystem, and pine forests flourish in higher elevations.	154
Visitors are warned that drinking water is limited in the park. They are also	168
told that gas is scarce and there are many wild animals. So, if you head to the	185
Spring Mountains – be prepared for anything.	191

Words Read:	Words Read:	Words Read:
minus mistakes:	minus mistakes:	minus mistakes:
equals cwpm:	equals cwpm:	equals cwpm:

Passage 25: Yellowstone

Jane and Bryan's parents were taking the family on their annual vacation.	12
They did an abundance of research and decided on Yellowstone National Park.	25
"We chose the location," Dad announced to the two as they finished up dinner	38
and started the dishes.	43
"It is up to you two to research and figure out what we are going to do while	61
we're there," Mom added.	65
Jane and Bryan went to work. They were visiting over spring break and would	78
have five days to fill. Jane made a list on her cell of things they wanted to do and	96
then they sorted them by importance.	104
"Old Faithful is a must do," Bryan said. "Listen to this: Old Faithful is a geyser.	119
It shoots boiling hot water into the air. It erupts every 44 minutes to 2 hours. Plus,	135
look at all of the hiking trails."	144
"Check and check. We also have to decide where to stay," Jane said.	157
"I vote for camping," Bryan announced loudly.	164
Janie sighed. "I'd think the lodge would be a better idea. A warm fire, four	179
walls, and no rocks under my back."	186
"Look! Cabins!" Bryan pointed to the screen.	193
"The perfect compromise!" Jane said. "We can hike and swim and go back	206
and take real showers."	210
"And go horseback riding."	214
"Sounds like a perfect trip. Let's go tell mom and dad!" they said together.	248

Words Read:	Words Read:	Words Read:
minus mistakes:	minus mistakes:	minus mistakes:
equals cwpm:	equals cwpm:	equals cwpm:

Name: _____

Passage 26: To the Lake

Mitchell didn't have a lot of money, but he wanted to take his girlfriend	15
someplace special to celebrate their anniversary.	21
"Why don't you take her to the lake?" Dad suggested.	31
"I'll pack you a picnic lunch," Mom added. "Dad, could you go out and get the	47
small ice chest and bring in a few sports drinks please?"	58
Mom and Dad were talking about Lake Tahoe. It was only a short drive up	73
Highway 50 and one of the family's favorite places to visit. Mitchell thought for a	87
moment and then nodded, thinking the idea was marvelous.	97
"I think that just may work," Mitchell said. "I'll text Tanner and tell her to bring	113
her suit."	115
"It may be a little cold for swimming," Mom said.	125
"But we can lay out after we eat," Mitchell said texting his girlfriend. "There's	139
nothing like the mix of warm sand and chilly air."	149
"I wanna go." Mitchell's little sister, Sammy, said as she came into the kitchen.	163
"Next time squirt," Mitchell said.	168
"How about you and I go for a bike ride?" Dad suggested as he began packing	183
the ice chest.	187
"The trail by the river?" Sammy asked.	194
"Your choice," Dad smiled.	198
"Do you want to come Mom?" Sammy asked.	206
"Sure, get my backpack. We'll have a picnic day for all," Mom smiled.	219
It was going to be a fun day. They were all lucky to live so close to such	237
amazing things to do.	241

Words Read:	Words Read:	Words Read:
minus mistakes:	minus mistakes:	minus mistakes:
equals cwpm:	equals cwpm:	equals cwpm:

Name: _____

Passage 27: Willow Smith

Willow Smith is an American singer and actress and the daughter of actors Will	14
Smith and Jada Pinkett Smith. She has received various accolades, including	25
a Young Artist Award, an NAACP Image Award, a BET Award, nominations for	38
two Daytime Emmy Awards and a coveted MTV Video Music Award.	49
In 2010, Willow signed with Jay-Z's recording label: Roc Nation. She is the	62
youngest artist Jay-Z has ever produced. Willow began her music career in 2010	75
with the release of "Whip My Hair," followed by "21st Century Girl" in 2011, and	90
the release of her first album on December 11, 2015. Willow has since released	104
multiple albums. Her songs often trend on TikTok.	112
Fun Facts: Willow's song "Summer Fling" is "...dedicated to all of the kids around	126
the world whose summer is never long enough."	134
Willow has acted with her father and has done voiceover work with her mother.	148
Willow was the voice of Baby Gloria in Madagascar: Escape 2 Africa. Her mother	162
voiced Older Gloria.	165
Have you ever done a major project with a family member? Willow has.	178

Words Read:	Words Read:	Words Read:
minus mistakes:	minus mistakes:	minus mistakes:
equals cwpm:	equals cwpm:	equals cwpm:

Passage 28: The Everglades

The Everglades is a unique and vast wetland located in southern Florida. It	13
covers more than 1.5 million acres, making it one of the largest wetlands in the	28
world. The Everglades is often called the "River of Grass" because it is a slow-	43
moving, shallow river filled with sawgrass marshes, swamps, and small islands.	54
This area is a special ecosystem with a mix of freshwater and saltwater, creating	68
a habitat for many different plants and animals.	76
The Everglades is home to a wide variety of wildlife. It's the only place on Earth	92
where both alligators and crocodiles live side by side. The wetlands also support	105
many species of fish, birds, turtles, and snakes. Some animals in the Everglades,	118
like the Florida panther and the West Indian manatee, are endangered. This	130
means there are very few of them left, and they are at risk of disappearing	145
forever. Protecting these animals and their habitat is important in order to keep	158
the ecosystem balanced.	161
The Everglades also plays a crucial role in providing clean water. The water	174
flows from a lake through the Everglades and eventually into the ocean, filtering	187
and purifying as it moves. This natural process helps maintain clean water	199
supplies for both humans and wildlife in Florida. However, the Everglades faces	211
many threats. Pollution, climate change, and development have harmed the	221
wetlands. Conservation efforts are underway to protect and restore the	231
Everglades so that it can continue to support wildlife and provide clean water.	244
This unique landscape is a valuable natural treasure worth preserving.	254

Words Read:	Words Read:	Words Read:
minus mistakes:	minus mistakes:	minus mistakes:
equals cwpm:	equals cwpm:	equals cwpm:

Passage 29: The History of Rugby

Rugby has a rich history, dating back to the early 19th century in England.   14

Legend has it that in 1823, a young student named William Webb Ellis, playing a   29

traditional game of football at Rugby School, picked up the ball and ran with it   44

toward the goal. This bold move is said to have inspired the creation of a new   60

sport, though there is little evidence to fully support this story. Nonetheless, the   73

town of Rugby became associated with the game, and over time, a set of rules   88

began to take shape.   92

In 1871, the Rugby Football Union (RFU) was formed in England to standardize   105

the game's rules. Soon after, rugby began to spread across the British Empire,   118

gaining popularity in countries like New Zealand, South Africa, and Australia. By   131

the early 20th century, rugby had split into two main forms: rugby union and   145

rugby league. Rugby union focuses on a more traditional, 15-player format, while   158

rugby league evolved into a faster-paced game with 13 players.   169

Rugby union was included in the Olympics in 1900, further raising the sport's   182

international profile. The Rugby World Cup, first held in 1987, is now one of the   197

world's largest sporting events, drawing teams from all over the globe. Today,   209

rugby is celebrated for its physicality, teamwork, and sense of sportsmanship,   220

with passionate fans and players found worldwide.   227

Words Read:	Words Read:	Words Read:
minus mistakes:	minus mistakes:	minus mistakes:
equals cwpm:	equals cwpm:	equals cwpm:

Reading 30: Frequency Word List 800

can't	matter	square	syllables	perhaps	5
bill	felt	suddenly	test	direction	10
center	farmers	ready	anything	divided	15
general	energy	subject	moon	region	20
return	dance	members	picked	simple	25
cells	paint	mind	love	cause	20
rain	exercise	eggs	train	blue	35
wish	drop	developed	window	difference	40
distance	sum	summer	wall	probably	45
legs	winter	wide	written	length	50
reason	kept	interest	brother	race	55
present	store	edge	past	sign	60
record	finished	discovered	wild	happy	65
beside	gone	sky	grass	million	70
west	lay	weather	root	instruments	75
meet	third	months	paragraph	raised	80
represent	soft	whether	clothes	flowers	85
shall	teacher	careless	chain	company	90
shoulder	fellow	crackers	season	soldier	95
ribbon	reason	shadow	spring	wrong	100

Words Read: _____	Words Read: _____	Words Read: _____
minus mistakes: _____	minus mistakes: _____	minus mistakes: _____
equals cwpm: _____	equals cwpm: _____	equals cwpm: _____

Reading 31: Frequency Word List 900

adverb	believe	bounce	cause	cells	5
command	complicate	dainty	den	develop	10
difference	direction	distance	divide	drag	15
energy	equals	Europe	example	exercise	20
feather	forest	friend	general	landscape	25
member	mind	misjudge	perhaps	possible	20
probably	produce	quickly	region	return	35
rhyme	rotation	scientist	simple	simply	40
site	square	subject	suddenly	syllables	45
synonym	window	another	answer	anyone	50
beautiful	beginning	cannot	clothes	different	55
doesn't	eighth	especially	everybody	except	60
excited	favorite	friend	getting	happily	65
loose	might	none	often	people	70
piece	terrible	through	tonight	usually	75
weather	whole	women	won't	wouldn't	80
writing	wrote	you're	lose	Wednesday	85
February	admire	align	guest	dessert	90
movable	light	dough	system	myth	95
thigh	pedal	patience	foreign	desert	100

Words Read: _____	Words Read: _____	Words Read: _____
minus mistakes: _____	minus mistakes: _____	minus mistakes: _____
equals cwpm: _____	equals cwpm: _____	equals cwpm: _____

Reading 32: Frequency Word List 1000

compromise	percent	advantage	coordinate	approve	5
additional	assembly	exploration	oppose	arctic	10
indicate	resistance	approach	origin	reveal	15
quiz	quotation	quality	adjust	classification	20
introduction	previous	constant	contribute	development	25
everyday	feedback	impact	logical	secondary	20
succession	achieve	define	maintain	severe	35
consist	lack	category	compact	composition	40
concern	dependent	depression	despite	detect	45
medium	obtain	relation	slightly	transition	50
version	attribute	engage	importance	mainly	55
preparation	recall	therefore	various	vast	60
accuracy	further	generally	highlight	navigation	65
neutral	presentation	propose	reliable	artificial	70
behave	confuse	constantly	demonstrate	desire	75
dominant	exert	gradually	informal	newly	80
promote	proportion	resolve	specialize	typical	85
contribution	convey	driven	encounter	farthest	90
incorrect	interaction	perspective	scarce	separation	95
suggestion	conjunction	irregular	assessment	understand	100

Words Read: _____ minus mistakes: _____ equals cwpm: _____	Words Read: _____ minus mistakes: _____ equals cwpm: _____	Words Read: _____ minus mistakes: _____ equals cwpm: _____

Set 3: 9th and 10th Grade Reading Level Passages - 1010L-1200L

Passage 33: Kobe Bryant

Basketball legend, Kobe Bryant, was born on August 23, 1978, in Philadelphia	12
Pennsylvania. During his professional basketball career with the Los Angeles	22
Lakers, Kobe was a five-time NBA Champion, a two-time finals MVP (most	36
valuable player), an 18-time NBA All-Star and a four-time NBA All-Star game	52
MVP.	53
Kobe's athletic ability was phenomenal. He was so talented that many believe	65
he was the greatest basketball player ever to grace the hardwood. Kobe was	78
special - one of a kind – with the maturity and skill to forgo college and enter	93
the NBA right out of high school. In 1996, Kobe became one of the elite few	109
players to enter the NBA draft from the twelfth grade. Kobe was selected the	123
13th overall draft pick and initially played for the Charlotte Hornets. The Hornets	136
subsequently traded Kobe to the Lakers.	142
Kobe was a high-flyer and fan favorite as a rookie. Kobe quickly became a	157
Los Angeles Lakers superstar. By 2004, Kobe was the cornerstone of the Los	170
Angeles Lakers. He led the team in scoring during 2005-06. He also led the team	186
in scoring during the 2006-07 season. His all-time career high was 81 points. That	200
was in one game. One. Game. Eighty-one is the second most points scored in	214
one game. Wilt Chamberlain holds the record for most points scored in a single	228
game – with 100-points in 1962.	234
In his last season of play, Kobe scored an NBA season-high 60 points	248
against Utah, outscoring the entire Jazz team 23–21 in the fourth quarter, in the	262
Lakers' 101–96 victory. He became the oldest player to score 60 or more points in	277
a game at 37 years and 234 days old. During his last time on the professional	293
stage, Kobe berated his opponents. His career culminated in typical Kobe	304
greatness.	305
Kobe met his tragic death in 2020 when he, his daughter, and seven others	318
died in a helicopter crash in Southern California.	326

Words Read: _____	Words Read: _____	Words Read: _____
minus mistakes: _____	minus mistakes: _____	minus mistakes: _____
equals cwpm: _____	equals cwpm: _____	equals cwpm: _____

Passage 34: Jade Carey

Jade Carey is an American gymnast known for her powerful and skillful	12
performances. Born on May 27, 2000, in Phoenix, Arizona, Jade showed talent in	25
gymnastics from a young age. She specializes in vault and floor exercises, where	38
her strength and precision have earned her a reputation as one of the top	52
gymnasts in the world. Jade's journey to the top of gymnastics has been marked	66
by hard work, determination, and a love for the sport.	76
In 2021, Jade achieved one of her biggest goals by representing the United	89
States at the Tokyo Olympics. Her performance was impressive and helped the	101
U.S. team succeed in a highly competitive field. In the individual events, Jade	114
won the gold medal on floor exercise, showing her incredible power, control, and	127
artistry. Her win made her one of the few American gymnasts to earn Olympic	141
gold in this event, and it solidified her place as one of the top gymnasts on the	157
world stage. Jade also competed in the 2024 Olympics, secured a bronze in	170
vault, and helped her teams towards gold in the team event.	181
Jade's success in gymnastics didn't come easily. She trained intensively with	192
her father, who is also her coach, and they worked together to build her skills	207
and routines. In addition to the Olympics, Jade has competed in various	219
international competitions, where she has won several medals for her strong	230
vaults and floor routines. Known for her dedication and humble personality,	241
Jade Carey continues to inspire young gymnasts around the world. Her	252
achievements highlight the rewards of hard work and the importance of	263
following one's dreams.	266

Words Read: _____	Words Read: _____	Words Read: _____
minus mistakes: _____	minus mistakes: _____	minus mistakes: _____
equals cwpm: _____	equals cwpm: _____	equals cwpm: _____

Name: _____

Passage 35: From F. Scott Fitzgerald's "The Great Gatsby"

There was music from my neighbor's house through the summer nights. In his	13
blue gardens men and girls came and went like moths among the whisperings	26
and the stars. At high tide in the afternoon, I watched his guests diving from the	42
tower of his raft or taking the sun on the hot sand of his beach while his two	60
motorboats slit the waters of the Sound.	67
On weekends his Rolls-Royce became a bus, bringing people to and from the	81
city between nine in the morning and long past midnight. This while his station	95
wagon scampered like a brisk yellow bug to meet all trains. And on Mondays	109
eight servants, including an extra gardener, worked all day with mops and	121
scrubbing-brushes and hammers and garden-shears, repairing the ravages of	132
the night before.	135
Every Friday five crates of oranges and lemons arrived from New York. Every	148
Monday these same oranges and lemons left his back door in a pyramid of	162
empty halves.	164
At least once a month a group of caterers came down with several hundred	178
feet of canvas and enough colored lights to make a Christmas tree of Gatsby's	192
enormous garden. On buffet tables, garnished with hors-d'oeuvre, spiced baked	203
hams crowded against salads and pork and turkeys golden brown.	213
By seven o'clock the orchestra has arrived, no thin five-piece affair, but a	227
whole group and trombones and saxophones and cornets and piccolos, and low	239
and high drums. The last swimmers have come in from the beach now and are	254
dressing upstairs; the cars from New York are parked five deep in the drive, and	269
already the halls and salons are fill of people.	278

Words Read: _____	Words Read: _____	Words Read: _____
minus mistakes: _____	minus mistakes: _____	minus mistakes: _____
equals cwpm: _____	equals cwpm: _____	equals cwpm: _____

Passage 36: Jane Bolin

Jane Bolin was a gifted attorney who became the first African American	12
female judge in the United States - serving on New York's Family Court for four	26
decades.	27
Jane Bolin was born in New York in 1908 to a British mother and an African	43
American father. This was unusual in 1908. Jane's mother died when Jane was	46
only 8-years-old. She was raised by her father, who was also an attorney and	72
distinguished scholar.	74
Jane was a brilliant student who graduated from high school two year early	87
and went on to enroll at Wellesley College. At Wellesley, Jane faced extreme	100
racism and social isolation, but she graduated with a Bachelor of Arts degree in	114
1928 and was officially recognized as one of the top students of her class. She	129
then attended Yale Law School, again facing social hostilities. She persevered	140
and graduated in 1931 becoming the first African-American woman to earn a	153
law degree from the institution.	158
Jane passed the bar in 1932 and went home to work with her father.	172
Jane wanted to go into politics. She ran for a state office but was	186
unsuccessful. Instead, she went to work as a corporate lawyer in New York City.	200
In 1939, the mayor of New York City appointed Jane to the position of judge of	216
the Domestic Relations Court.	220
Jane was a thoughtful judge. She was a child and race advocate and worked	234
to better the plight of children. She also confronted a range of domestic issues.	248
She worked to change segregationist policies within the court and probation	259
systems, including ending skin-color-based assignments for probation officers.	269
Additionally, Jane worked with first lady Eleanor Roosevelt to create a school to	282
help lower juvenile crime rates among boys.	289
Jane retired from the bench at the age of 70 and went to work as a	305
consultant and school-based volunteer. Jane died in Long Island City, Queens,	317
New York, on January 8, 2007. She was 98.	326

Words Read: _____	Words Read: _____	Words Read: _____
minus mistakes: _____	minus mistakes: _____	minus mistakes: _____
equals cwpm: _____	equals cwpm: _____	equals cwpm: _____

Passage 37: Video Games are Big Business

As one of the best-selling toys ever - video games are big business. From	14
early games to new titles, millions of dollars a year are spent on video games.	29
Mass market sales of games began in the 1970s and have increased	41
exponentially year after year after year. In a crowded field of fan favorites –	54
what video games are the all-time best sellers?	63
The Mario series is one of the gaming industries most successful and	74
renowned franchises in history - with many of its titles, particularly within	86
the *Super Mario* subseries, being considered the greatest video games ever	97
made. Mario is the best-selling video game franchise of all time, with more than	112
776 million copies of games sold, including more than 390 million for the *Super*	126
Mario games alone. This makes Mario one of the highest-grossing media	138
franchises of all time. Introduced in 1981, Nintendo has made over $32.4 billion	151
on that franchise to date.	156
In 1996, *Pokémon* took over the market. Originally played on Gameboy, the	168
Pokémon franchise has made about $20 billion dollars. For Nintendo once	179
again, and like Mario, Pokémon has released several generations of games.	190
Continual updates and a wide variety of console versions have made this	202
franchise second only to its Italian plumber brothers and their friends.	213
Older games, like *Pac-Man* and *Space Invaders*, also made the best seller list.	226
The staying power of Pac-Man has made its publishers $14 billion to date. Space	241
Invaders, from 1978, has made Atari about $13 billion – from Space Invaders!	253
Other titles rounding out the list of winsome and popular games, but not	266
really coming close to the big two, include Minecraft, Tetris, Grand Theft Auto,	279
and Wii Sport.	282
What's your favorite video game?	287

Words Read: _____	Words Read: _____	Words Read: _____
minus mistakes: _____	minus mistakes: _____	minus mistakes: _____
equals cwpm: _____	equals cwpm: _____	equals cwpm: _____

Passage 38: Why Does Napoleon Matter?

Napoleon Bonaparte was a French military and political leader who rose to	12
prominence during the French Revolution. Napoleon was born on the island of	24
Corsica in 1769. He was the emperor of France twice - once from May 1804 to	39
April 1814 and again from March 1815 to June 1815. Today, Napoleon is	52
considered one of the greatest military generals in history. He is also one of the	67
most significant people in history according to the United Kingdom Sunday	78
Times and Time Magazine. Both publications developed computer algorithms to	88
compile their lists.	91
Napoleon rose to prominence in the last days of the French Revolution by	104
conquering much of Europe. He made France the preeminent power of the	116
region until he was defeated at the Battle of Waterloo in 1815.	128
His legacy is not untarnished and is the subject of much debate. Many argue	142
he was a volatile and evil dictator while others label the fallen general a	156
visionary and a hero.	160
His legal reforms were far reaching. His Code Napoleon, or Napoleonic Codes,	172
made all men equal under the law and formed the bases for civil codes across	187
the world.	189
Dictator or hero – there is not one library or museum named or fashioned	202
after Napoleon. He did not die a hero but was exiled to a remote island in the	219
South Pacific where he died of cancer at the age of 51.	231
Napoleon was a man of many words and is often quoted. Some of his quotes	246
include:	247
"Never interrupt your enemy when he is making a mistake."	257
"Envy is a declaration of inferiority."	263
"The reason people fail instead of succeed is they trade what they want most	277
for what they want at the moment."	284

Words Read: _____	Words Read: _____	Words Read: _____
minus mistakes: _____	minus mistakes: _____	minus mistakes: _____
equals cwpm: _____	equals cwpm: _____	equals cwpm: _____

Passage 39: Albert Einstein

Albert Einstein just may be the most influential scientists of the 21st century.	13
His theory of relativity changed our understanding of space, time, gravity, and	25
the universe. Additionally, he set the scientific foundations for everything from	36
paper towels to lasers.	40

Paper towels? That's right, paper towels.   46

The Scott Paper Company is often credited with the invention of this item now   60
found in every household in America; however, the first physics article Einstein   72
ever published was one in which he analyzed wicking – which – in turn – led the   86
way to the development of paper towels.   93

Wicking is the phenomenon that allows paper towels to soak up liquids when   106
gravity wants to drag the fluid downward. This process is also what pulls hot   120
wax into a candle wick, hence the term "wick," as in wicking. This "wicking" is   135
known as a capillary action. It is also the science behind how sap rises in trees   151
as well as keeps ink lower into the top of an ink pen. Einstein's paper was   167
published in 1901. It was controversial at the time. The idea of atoms and   181
molecules were in and of themselves controversial.   188

The paper demonstrated Einstein was open to analysis and study of atoms   200
and molecules. This turned heads because Einstein was siding with radical   211
physicists who believed this capillary action was just one of many phenomena   223
that was explainable by the way atoms and molecules interact, and it was!   236

Einstein worked on this wicking theory for years. By 1905, he'd developed an   249
equation that described the math behind the theory. This paper not only gave us   263
the science for paper towels – it was the first incontrovertible proof that atoms   276
and molecules existed.   279

Einstein's legacy is long and storied and one that makes our lives easier   292
everyday – whether we know it or not.   299

Words Read: _____	Words Read: _____	Words Read: _____
minus mistakes: _____	minus mistakes: _____	minus mistakes: _____
equals cwpm: _____	equals cwpm: _____	equals cwpm: _____

Passage 40: From Little Women by Louisa May Alcott

"Christmas won't be Christmas without any presents," grumbled Jo, lying on	11
the rug.	13
"It's so dreadful to be poor!" sighed Meg, looking down at her old dress.	27
"I don't think it's fair for some girls to have plenty of pretty things, and other	43
girls nothing at all," added little Amy, with an injured sniff.	54
"We've got Father and Mother, and each other," said Beth contentedly from	66
her corner.	68
The four young faces on which the firelight shone brightened at the cheerful	81
words, but darkened again as Jo said sadly, "We haven't got Father, and shall	95
not have him for a long time." She didn't say "perhaps never," but each silently	110
added it, thinking of Father far away, where the fighting was.	121
Nobody spoke for a minute; then Meg said in an altered tone, "You know the	136
reason Mother proposed not having any presents this Christmas was because it	148
is going to be a hard winter for everyone; and she thinks we ought not to spend	165
money for pleasure, when our men are suffering so in the army. We can't do	180
much, but we can make our little sacrifices, and ought to do it gladly. But I am	197
afraid I don't," and Meg shook her head, as she thought regretfully of all the	212
pretty things she wanted.	216
"But I don't think the little we should spend would do any good. We've each	231
got a dollar, and the army wouldn't be much helped by our giving that. I agree	247
not to expect anything from Mother or you, but I do want to buy a special book	264
for myself. I've wanted it so long," said Jo, who was a bookworm.	277
"I planned to spend mine in new music," said Beth, with a little sigh, which no	293
one heard but the hearth brush and kettle-holder.	303
"I shall get a nice box of Faber's drawing pencils; I really need them," said	318
Amy decidedly.	320

Words Read: _____	Words Read: _____	Words Read: _____
minus mistakes: _____	minus mistakes: _____	minus mistakes: _____
equals cwpm: _____	equals cwpm: _____	equals cwpm: _____

Passage 41: Dr. J

Dr. J was born Julius Erving on February 22, 1950. Dr. J is a former	15
professional basketball player who is regarded as one of the most talented and	28
influential players of all time. Dr. J was instrumental in legitimizing the American	41
Basketball Association and he was the best-known player in that league when it	55
merged with the National Basketball Association in 1976.	63

Dr. J won three league championships, four Most Valuable Player Awards, — 74
along with many other achievements. No team he played on ever missed — 86
postseason. He is the eighth highest scorer of all time with an astounding 30,026 — 100
points over his sixteen years of play. — 107

Best known by fans for dunking from the free-throw line, Dr. J was inducted — 122
into the Basketball Hall of Fame in 1994. Julius Erving is the player who brought — 137
dunking to the forefront when he played with the Philadelphia 76ers. Dr. J put — 151
artistry into many shots including in the 1980 NBA Finals game against the Los — 165
Angeles Lakers when he executed the legendary "Baseline Move" – a behind the — 177
board reverse layup. This shot went down as one of the most spectacular shots — 191
in basketball history. — 194

Magic Johnson was a rookie and recalled the shot in a Times interview: "Here — 208
I was, trying to win a championship, and my mouth just dropped open. He — 222
actually did that, I thought – what should we do? Should we take the ball out or — 238
should we ask him to do it again?" — 246

The 76ers lost the game, but the 1980-81 season was Dr. J's greatest — 258
individual year. — 260

Dr. J retired at age 37. Since his retirement, he has fashioned himself a — 274
brilliant businessman and basketball executive. — 279

Words Read: _____	Words Read: _____	Words Read: _____
minus mistakes: _____	minus mistakes: _____	minus mistakes: _____
equals cwpm: _____	equals cwpm: _____	equals cwpm: _____

Name: _____

Passage 42: The Avengers

Fifty-five years ago, a book hit shelves that would define an entire generation | 14
of superheroes to their fans. Jack Kirby and Stan Lee didn't invent the idea of | 29
the cape-and-cowl team-up with Avengers #1 back in 1963, but they certainly | 44
changed it forever — all without knowing that they were planting the seeds for | 57
what would eventually blossom into one of the biggest multimedia franchises on | 69
earth. The question is: Does that first issue still hold up after all these years? | 84

It may be historically important, but is Avengers #1 actually a good comic? | 97
It's safe to say just about everyone has at least some idea how the Avengers | 112
were formed. This is thanks to the mega-Marvel Cinematic Franchise. The | 124
concept itself isn't complicated: A group of independent superheroes come | 134
together for the first time, form a team, and decide to stay together – but each | 149
also fights crime on their own if need be. | 158

In Avenger's #1 – the comic - Thor's brother Loki is cast to an island for his | 173
wrongdoing. Loki devises a plan to get back at Thor. Loki uses the Hulk as a | 189
pawn and the Fantastic Four come to the rescue. After much drama, and much | 203
more action, the dust settles, and the heroes are victorious. Then, Hank Pym sells | 217
the idea of a team. "Each of us has a different power, if we combined forces, we | 234
could be almost unbeatable!" No one — not even Hulk — needs much more in the | 248
way of convincing. So, it's settled. Unceremonious as it may be, they're a team - | 262
though as Iron Man explains they'll "fight together or separately, if need be," so | 276
the whole team thing is left open ended. They call themselves the Avengers. The | 290
rest is history. | 293

Is Avengers #1 a good comic? Probably not by modern standards —but at the | 307
end of the day, that hardly matters; because Avengers #1 is emblematic of an | 321
era of comics that reads as irreconcilably campy but not without value. There's a | 335
showmanship in them that can be felt all these decades later. It's the spirit of | 350
the thing, more than the practice. And isn't that what matters most anyway? | 363

Words Read: _____	Words Read: _____	Words Read: _____
minus mistakes: _____	minus mistakes: _____	minus mistakes: _____
equals cwpm: _____	equals cwpm: _____	equals cwpm: _____

on

Name: _____

Passage 43: The Crow, an Inuit Tale

In a land full of rivers, mountains, lakes, and forest animals, indigenous people | 13
have traditionally used folk tales to pass down traditions. These stories endured | 25
through generations and are an extraordinarily fascinating aspect of Native | 35
American culture. *Crow Brings Daylight* is one of those stories. | 45

Crow Brings Daylight is a myth of the Inuit people who lived and still live in the | 62
northernmost parts of North America. | 67

Long ago, when the world was still new, the Inuit lived in the darkness of their | 83
home farther north than light would travel. The people had never heard of | 96
daylight until Crow came upon them and told them of the brilliance of daylight – | 110
even then - they did not believe him. | 117

The older Intuits would not listen, but the younger generations were intrigued. | 129
They made Crow repeat his tales until they'd memorized every word. | 140

"Imagine how much easier hunting and fishing would be," one said. | 151

"Yes, and the advantage of seeing a polar bear before he attacks," replied | 164
another. | 165

Soon the youthful yearning for daylight was so strong they begged Crow to | 178
bring it back with him. Crow was old and tired. He did not know if he could make | 196
the journey, but he longed to help the Inuit live under the light. | 209

Crow flew for many miles through the endless darkness of the north. He | 222
strained his wings and flew with all his might. Suddenly, the daylight world burst | 236
upon him and the endless shades of color and the many shapes and forms | 250
surrounding him made Crow stare in wonder. Above him, the sky was an endless | 264
blue, the clouds fluffy and white. | 270

He came upon a village in the sun and followed a young girl into the chieftain's | 286
hut by turning himself into a speck of dust. He floated into a child's ear and told | 303
her to play with the orbs of light that were in a box in the hut, and then to bring | 322
one outside. Then Crow changed himself back and took the ball of light in his | 337
beak and flew back North. Once there, the orb shattered on the ground and gave | 352
the Inuit people daylight. However, Crow was old and tired, he said that he must | 367
rest every six months before bringing the light again. Even so, the journeys | 380
shortened crow's life, but he did it for the people. So, the Inuit people have six | 396
months of daylight and six months of darkness, and they are always kind to Crow. | 411

Words Read:	Words Read:	Words Read:
minus mistakes:	minus mistakes:	minus mistakes:
equals cwpm:	equals cwpm:	equals cwpm:

Passage 44: Acadia National Park

Established in 1919, Acadia National Park is home to hiking, fishing, biking,	12
camping and some of the most beautiful land and seascapes in the world.	25
Acadia is a 47,000-acre Atlantic coast recreation area on Maine's Mount	36
Desert Island and the first national park east of the Mississippi River. The park	50
also encompasses and preserves part of the Isle au Haut, the tip of the Schoodic	65
Peninsula, and 16 smaller outlying islands. It protects the natural beauty of the	78
rocky headlands, including the highest mountains along the Atlantic coast	88
including Cadillac Mountain. Cadillac Mountain is 1,530 feet above sea level.	99
Acadia features a glaciated coastal and island landscape, an abundance of	110
habitats, rich biodiversity, clean air and water, and a fascinating cultural	121
heritage.	122
The park is 6000 acres. There are more than 130 miles of hiking trails and 45	138
miles of carriage roads. The historic carriage roads are 16 feet wide and	151
considered the best example of broken stone roads in the United States. They are	164
a hand-honed engineering wonder.	170
Acadia is known for many things. It is the best place on the east coast to see	187
the Milky Way but bring a jacket because the average temperature in Coastal	200
Maine is 44.3 degrees Fahrenheit.	205
The park is home to over 1,500 species of birds, plants and animals. If you are	220
ever in Maine – Acadia National Park is a must see.	231

Words Read:	Words Read:	Words Read:
minus mistakes:	minus mistakes:	minus mistakes:
equals cwpm:	equals cwpm:	equals cwpm:

Passage 45: Arches National Park in Utah

Arches National Park, in Moab, Utah, gets its name from the over 2,000	13
natural stone arches that make up the park's breathtaking landscape. The park	25
has over 2,000 natural stone arches, hundreds of soaring pinnacles, massive rock	36
fins, and giant balanced rocks. This park is a red-rock nirvana with inspirational	50
sunsets and spectacular landscapes.	55
The park is tremendously poplar with a list of must-sees that include the	68
Delicate Arch whose picture graces Utah license plates and a massive collection	81
of artwork. The Landscape arch is a park-goer's favorite. It is a delicate, 290-	96
foot sandstone spiderweb and an easy 0.8 hike from the Devil's Garden Trailhead	108
– with plenty of arches to see along the way.	118
There are many other must-sees and a plethora of things to do. At Arches	133
National Park you can ATV, backpack, camp, hike and climb. There is river rafting	146
and mountain biking. One thing you can't do is take home rocks.	159
The park is part of the National Park Service and was originally named	172
a national monument on April 12, 1929. It was redesignated as a national park on	186
November 12, 1971. The park receives more than 1.6 million visitors annually.	199

Words Read:	Words Read:	Words Read:
minus mistakes:	minus mistakes:	minus mistakes:
equals cwpm:	equals cwpm:	equals cwpm:

Passage 46: Kylie Jenner

Kylie Jenner is a social media superstar with millions of followers, dozens of	13
brand deals, and her own product lines. The young entrepreneur has made a	26
fortune selling her own make-up and fashion lines. Kylie is so popular that *Time*	41
Magazine recently named her the most influential influencer of all time. She is so	55
influential that when she tweeted she'd lost interest in Snapchat – the platform's	67
revenue dropped 1 billion dollars in value. When Kylie speaks, people listen.	79
When Kylie was fourteen, she and her sister teamed up with the PacSun	92
clothing store to create *The Kendell and Kylie* Collection. The line was a massive	106
success. From there Kylie launched a jewelry line and teamed with nail polish	119
manufacturer OPI to create her own colors. She promoted the brand and sales	132
skyrocketed.	133
Kylie uses her clout for philanthropy as well. The young super-influencer set	146
up an eBay account to sell her clothes, shoes and bags to benefit the Los Angeles	162
Children's Hospital.	164
In 2015, Kendell and Kylie launched a clothing line with the British company	177
Topshop. The line includes swimsuits and summer wear.	185
By February 2016, Kylie'd launched her own make-up company called Kylie	197
Cosmetics. In May of the same year, she released her first rap single.	210
And she's nice. When a high school junior in Sacramento, California asked her	223
to go to his prom, she said yes. Imagine the surprise when Kylie showed up a Rio	240
Americano High School for prom.	245
What do you know about Kylie Jenner?	252

Words Read:	Words Read:	Words Read:
minus mistakes:	minus mistakes:	minus mistakes:
equals cwpm:	equals cwpm:	equals cwpm:

Passage 47: The WNBA

The WNBA, Women's National Basketball Association, began on April 22, 1996,	11
with an announcement from basketball greats Rebecca Lobo, Lisa Leslie, and	22
Sheryl Swoops. The first game was played on June 21, 1997, in Los Angeles,	36
California between the L.A. Sparks and the New York Liberty. With a crowd of	50
14,284 in attendance, New York took the first win in league history. Today there	64
are more than 10 million WNBA fans.	71
Eight teams made up the first season – with four in the Eastern Conference and	84
four in the Western Conference. The first president of the WNBA was Val	98
Ackerman, and Sheryl Swoops was the first player signed to the league. Today,	111
there are 12 league teams that play the regular season from May to September	125
and the finals into October.	130
Each WNBA team plays 36 games - eighteen are played at home and 18 are	144
played away. Each team hosts and visits every other team at least once every	158
season - just like the NBA.	163

Words Read:	Words Read:	Words Read:
minus mistakes:	minus mistakes:	minus mistakes:
equals cwpm:	equals cwpm:	equals cwpm:

Passage 48: Troy Aikman

Troy Aikman is known as one of the best quarterbacks in NFL history. He	14
played for the Dallas Cowboys and helped lead them to great success. Born on	28
November 21, 1966, in West Covina, California, Aikman first played college	39
football at the University of Oklahoma, then transferred to UCLA. In 1989, he was	53
the first overall pick in the NFL Draft, chosen by the Cowboys. This began his	68
impressive NFL career.	71
Aikman's first few seasons with the Cowboys were difficult, but he soon helped	84
turn the team around. His calm leadership, accurate throws, and strong arm were	97
key to the Cowboys' success in the 1990s. With Aikman at quarterback, the	110
Cowboys won three Super Bowl championships in just four years—in 1992, 1993,	123
and 1995. In the 1993 Super Bowl, Aikman was named MVP, showing his	136
importance to the team.	140
Aikman's skill made him a tough opponent. He was known for his connection	153
with teammates like Emmitt Smith and Michael Irvin, forming an offense that was	166
hard to beat. By the time he retired in 2000, Aikman had over 32,000 passing	181
yards and 165 touchdowns. His legacy as a Dallas Cowboys legend and a Hall of	196
Fame quarterback remains strong.	200
After football, Aikman became a sports broadcaster, bringing his knowledge to	211
fans watching from home. His career in broadcasting has kept him close to the	225
game. Today, he is remembered both for his achievements on the field and for his	240
contributions to the NFL as an analyst.	247

Words Read:	Words Read:	Words Read:
minus mistakes:	minus mistakes:	minus mistakes:
equals cwpm:	equals cwpm:	equals cwpm:

Passage 49: Nova Scotia

Nova Scotia is a beautiful province on the east coast of Canada. It is one of	16
the country's three Maritime provinces and is almost completely surrounded by	27
the Atlantic Ocean. Nova Scotia is known for its stunning coastlines, rolling hills,	40
and historic towns. The province includes over 3,000 small islands and has many	53
beaches, coves, and bays. Its location along the ocean has shaped much of its	67
history and culture, especially through fishing, sailing, and shipbuilding.	76
The capital city of Nova Scotia is Halifax, which is known for its lively	90
waterfront, historic sites, and friendly atmosphere. Halifax has a deep harbor and	102
was an important port in both world wars. Today, it remains a popular spot for	117
visitors with its museums, parks, and seafood restaurants. Other well-known	128
places in Nova Scotia include Cape Breton Island, famous for its scenic Cabot	141
Trail, and the Bay of Fundy, which has the highest tides in the world. The tides	157
here can rise over 50 feet, creating a dramatic natural show every day.	170
Nova Scotia has a rich cultural heritage influenced by Indigenous people, as	182
well as early settlers from Scotland, France, and England. This mix of cultures can	196
still be seen today in local festivals, music, and food. Many people visit Nova	210
Scotia to experience its unique blend of natural beauty and history. Whether	222
exploring coastal villages, hiking trails, or enjoying fresh seafood, Nova Scotia	233
offers a warm and welcoming experience for all who visit.	243

Words Read:	Words Read:	Words Read:
minus mistakes:	minus mistakes:	minus mistakes:
equals cwpm:	equals cwpm:	equals cwpm:

Passage 50: 21 Savage

21 Savage was born in 1992. He is a British-American rapper known for his	15
gritty, street-inspired lyrics and unique sound. Growing up in a tough	27
neighborhood in Atlanta, Georgia, he faced many challenges from a young age.	39
These challenges shaped his music. His career took off in 2015 with the release of	54
his debut mixtape, *The Slaughter Tape*. This debut introduced fans to his raw,	67
unfiltered style.	69
21 Savage gained mainstream recognition with his 2016 collaboration with	79
producer Metro Boomin on the EP *Savage Mode*. The EP's success was fueled by	93
hit tracks like "No Heart" and "X." These tracks showcased his dark, haunting	106
beats and straightforward delivery. His first studio album, *Issa Album* was	116
released in 2017. It included the single "Bank Account," which became a major hit	131
and cemented his place in the rap industry.	139
Beyond music, 21 Savage is known for his philanthropy, particularly around	150
financial literacy and community empowerment. In 2018, he launched the *21*	161
Savage Bank Account Campaign, aimed at teaching young people about	171
managing money. He has also been vocal about social justice issues, drawing	183
from his own experiences.	187
In 2019, 21 Savage's immigration status became a national topic when he was	200
detained by U.S. Immigration and Customs Enforcement (ICE). He was revealed	211
to be a British citizen, bringing more attention to the struggles faced by	224
immigrants in the U.S. Today. 21 Savage continues to be influential both in the	238
music world and in his community.	244

Words Read:	Words Read:	Words Read:
minus mistakes:	minus mistakes:	minus mistakes:
equals cwpm:	equals cwpm:	equals cwpm:

Passage 51: Mark Cuban

Mark Cuban is a well-known entrepreneur, investor, and television personality.	11
Born in 1958 in Pittsburgh, Pennsylvania, Cuban was interested in business from a	24
young age. At 12, he started selling garbage bags to make extra money, and he	39
continued to work different jobs through high school and college. Cuban attended	51
Indiana University, where he studied business and began developing his	61
entrepreneurial skills.	63
After college, he moved to Dallas, Texas, and started his first business,	75
MicroSolutions, a computer software company. Cuban's company grew quickly,	84
and he sold it in 1990, making a large profit. In 1995, he co-founded	99
Broadcast.com, an internet radio company. Just a few years later, he sold	111
Broadcast.com to Yahoo! for billions of dollars, making him a billionaire.	122
In 2000, Cuban bought the Dallas Mavericks, a professional basketball team.	133
Under his ownership, the Mavericks improved and won their first NBA	144
championship in 2011. Cuban is known for his passion for the team and often sits	159
courtside at games, cheering them on.	165
Today, Mark Cuban is also a "shark" investor on the TV show Shark Tank. He	180
listens to business pitches and invests in ideas he believes in. Cuban is admired	194
for his business knowledge, bold personality, and commitment to helping new	205
entrepreneurs succeed. He continues to be a major influence in the world of	218
business and sports.	221

Words Read:	Words Read:	Words Read:
minus mistakes:	minus mistakes:	minus mistakes:
equals cwpm:	equals cwpm:	equals cwpm:

Passage 52: Broadcast.com

Broadcast.com was an internet radio company that became famous in the late	13
1990s. It started in 1995, when Mark Cuban and his friend Todd Wagner saw a	28
new opportunity in online media. They wanted to help people listen to live sports	42
and events over the internet, which was a new idea at the time. Before streaming	57
services like Spotify or YouTube existed, Broadcast.com allowed people to listen	68
to radio stations, news, and even live sports games online.	78
The company grew quickly as more people began using the internet.	89
Broadcast.com offered live streaming of major events, from sports games to	100
special interviews, giving people access to events they couldn't otherwise	110
experience. This caught the attention of big companies interested in digital	121
media.	122
In 1999, Yahoo! saw potential in Broadcast.com and bought it for $5.7 billion,	135
making it one of the biggest internet deals of that time. The sale turned Mark	150
Cuban into a billionaire. However, as technology changed, Yahoo! faced	160
challenges in keeping up with new streaming services. Broadcast.com eventually	170
closed down, but it paved the way for future online media platforms.	182
Today, Broadcast.com is remembered as one of the early pioneers of internet	194
streaming. It showed how digital media could connect people to live events and	207
entertainment online, opening doors for today's streaming giants.	215

Words Read:	Words Read:	Words Read:
minus mistakes:	minus mistakes:	minus mistakes:
equals cwpm:	equals cwpm:	equals cwpm:

Reading 53: Frequency Word List 1100

analysis	absolute	variation	academic	conjecture	5
association	interval	standardize	initial	percentage	10
approximate	translate	modify	randomly	conditional	15
periodic	approximately	objective	appeal	cite	20
principle	statistics	assess	verify	experimental	25
universal	alternate	annual	effective	integration	20
satisfy	arrangement	calculation	extension	trend	35
assign	noble	thus	indirect	enable	40
emphasize	paraphrase	participate	aspect	continuous	45
compose	insight	enlarge	consult	interpretation	50
complement	distinct	instance	distinguish	format	55
distribute	synthesize	verbal	downward	margin	60
slant	dynamic	significant	confirm	valid	65
brainstorm	external	prior	restate	effectively	70
operate	fundamental	peer	isolate	greatly	75
accurately	commonly	dramatic	frequently	logically	80
singular	advertise	apparent	span	similarly	85
insert	climax	educate	imply	achievement	90
creative	boldface	informative	properly	ensure	95
fully	analogy	assumption	restrict	occupy	100

Words Read: _____ minus mistakes: _____ equals cwpm: _____	Words Read: _____ minus mistakes: _____ equals cwpm: _____	Words Read: _____ minus mistakes: _____ equals cwpm: _____

Reading 54: Frequency Word List Level 1100 B

regard	regard	complicate	enclose	intend	5
optical	intensity	tendency	virtual	admire	10
conversion	inductively	rapid	respectively	yield	15
breed	cumulative	subordinate	suspect	chronological	20
continuously	efficiency	undergo	categorize	rearrange	25
typically	update	revision	usage	derive	20
overlap	consistent	criteria	integrate	multimedia	35
atmospheric	explanatory	literacy	practical	resemble	40
widely	descend	improvement	obstacle	publication	45
simulate	briefly	highly	fascinate	hypothesize	50
precede	employ	restriction	anecdote	rubric	55
speculate	currently	limitation	meaningful	regularly	60
relatively	tightly	dominate	gender	participant	65
requirement	sufficient	circumstance	fictional	passive	70
specify	technical	acquire	logic	mythological	75
recreation	unfold	exposition	inductive	scheme	80
timeline	consequence	factual	astronomy	characterize	85
evolve	focal	quantitative	alter	donate	90
functional	observational	collaboration	comparative	fame	95
finite	spun	caution	donate	exhaust	100

Words Read: _____ minus mistakes: _____ equals cwpm: _____	Words Read: _____ minus mistakes: _____ equals cwpm: _____	Words Read: _____ minus mistakes: _____ equals cwpm: _____

Reading 55: Frequency Word List Level 1100 C

exhaust	qualitative	symbolic	align	convenient	5
manipulate	propel	shield	significance	somewhat	10
exceed	exception	incomplete	keyword	originate	15
outward	reduction	unexpected	capitalize	destructive	20
occurrence	quest	rarely	steadily	symbolize	25
adequate	afterward	analytical	anticipate	classical	20
complexity	freely	impress	interfere	memorable	35
narration	numerous	partly	slight	suspend	40
thrive	deeply	enhance	favorable	motivation	45
regularly	thoroughly	uncover	vague	contradiction	50
install	regulation	smoothly	technology	visually	55
brightly	annually	displace	excess	introductory	60
regardless	reinforce	repel	shortage	spite	65
suitable	worldwide	fitness	selective	separately	70
vital	exposure	likewise	minimize	partially	75
perceive	portable	abbreviation	converge	determination	80
flaw	mislead	persuasion	roughly	unbiased	85
unchanged	coherent	effectiveness	efficiently	incorporate	90
yearly	contrast	narratee	legendary	mandatory	95
omit	quote	candor	cause	eligible	100

Words Read: _____	Words Read: _____	Words Read: _____
minus mistakes: _____	minus mistakes: _____	minus mistakes: _____
equals cwpm: _____	equals cwpm: _____	equals cwpm: _____

Set 4: 12th Grade Reading Level Passages - 1210L-1400L

Passage 56: Tom Brady

Passage 57: Northern Lights

Passage 58: The Parker Space Probe

Passage 59: Karl Mark

Passage 60: From Alice's Adventures in Wonderland by Lewis Carroll

Passage 61: Relativity by Albert Einstein

Passage 62: The 19th Amendment and Voting Rights

Passage 63: From George Orwell's Animal Farm

Passage 64: What Plants Are

Passage 65: The Gettysburg Address

Passage 66: Yosemite

Passage 67: Kobe Bryant 2

Passage 68: Elle Fanning

Passage 69: Gal Gadot

Passage 70: Carissa Moore– Champion of the Waves

Passage 71: Alex Morgan – Soccer Trailblazer

Passage 72: Dalilah Muhammad Hurdler

Passage 73: Makenzie Ziegler – Fact and Opinion

Passage 74: The History of Hershey

Passage 75: Jack Dylan Grazer

Passage 76: Bradley Cooper

Passage 77: Six Flags

Reading 78: Word List 1200

Reading 79: Word List 1300

Reading 80: Word List 1400

Name: _____

Passage 56: Tom Brady

Tom Brady is widely regarded as one of the greatest quarterbacks in NFL	13
history. Born on August 3, 1977, in San Mateo, California, he played college	26
football at the University of Michigan before entering the NFL. In the 2000 NFL	40
Draft, the New England Patriots selected him in the sixth round, a decision that	54
would prove monumental for both Brady and the team. Although his career	66
started slowly, Brady quickly emerged as a star.	74
In 2001, he became the Patriots' starting quarterback and led them to a Super	88
Bowl victory that season. This was the first of many championships for Brady,	101
who would go on to win six Super Bowl titles with the Patriots. Known for his	117
leadership, work ethic, and incredible skill, Brady earned admiration from fans	128
and teammates alike.	131
In 2020, Brady made a surprising move by joining the Tampa Bay Buccaneers.	144
Many doubted whether he could succeed with a new team, especially at his age.	158
However, he silenced critics by leading the Buccaneers to a Super Bowl victory in	172
2021, earning his seventh Super Bowl ring—the most by any player in NFL history.	187
Over his career, Brady has broken numerous NFL records, including those for	199
Super Bowl appearances, passing touchdowns, and passing yards. His continued	209
success defies the typical limitations of age in professional sports, inspiring fans	221
and young players around the world. Tom Brady's story is one of resilience,	234
dedication, and a relentless pursuit of excellence, securing his legacy as one of	247
the all-time greats in football.	253

Words Read:	Words Read:	Words Read:
minus mistakes:	minus mistakes:	minus mistakes:
equals cwpm:	equals cwpm:	equals cwpm:

Passage 57: The Northern Lights

Aurora borealis, more commonly known as the northern lights, are an	11
atmospheric phenomenon that lights up the sky at the top off the world. The	25
aurora borealis are dancing waves of cerulean and emerald waves of light	37
formed from the violent depths of nature.	44
The northern lights shine when energized particles from the sun collide into	56
the Earth's upper atmosphere at speeds of over 45 million mph. Earth's	68
magnetic field protects us from its force by redirecting the particles towards the	81
poles.	82
Billy Teets, director of the Dyer Observatory at Vanderbilt University in	93
Nashville, Tennessee explains it like this. "These particles are deflected towards	104
the poles of the earth by our planet's magnetic field and interact with our	118
atmosphere, depositing energy and causing the atmosphere to fluoresce."	127
The bright colors of the northern lights are caused by the chemical	139
composition of Earth's atmosphere.	143
"Every type of atom or molecule, whether it's atomic hydrogen or a molecule	156
like carbon dioxide, absorbs and radiates its own unique set of colors, which is	170
analogous to how every human being has a unique set of fingerprints," Teets	183
continued. "Some of the dominant colors seen in aurora are red, a hue produced	197
by the nitrogen molecules, and green, which is produced by oxygen molecules."	209
Explorers and adventurers have been in awe of the Northern Lights for years,	222
but scientists at NASA are still looking for clues about how they work. In 2018,	237
NASA launched the Parker Solar Probe. Part of its mission is to collect	250
information that could tell us more about the northern lights.	260
Did you know there are southern lights too? They are called the southern	273
lights or aurora australis.	277

Words Read: _____	Words Read: _____	Words Read: _____
minus mistakes: _____	minus mistakes: _____	minus mistakes: _____
equals cwpm: _____	equals cwpm: _____	equals cwpm: _____

Passage 58: The Parker Space Probe

On August 12, 2018, NASA launched the Parker Space Probe aboard a United	13
Launch Alliance Delta IV heavy rocket. The mission of the Parker Space Probe is	27
to study the sun in more detail than ever before.	37

The Parker was the first spacecraft ever to "touch" the sun when it slipped 51
inside the sun's outer atmosphere, or corona, on April 28, 2021. On the probe's 65
mission, it will complete 24 orbits of the sun over seven years and will fly over 71
seven times closer to our star than any other spacecraft. 81

NASA hopes the probe will answer questions about solar physics that have 93
baffled them for over six decades. According to NASA, during the probes closest 106
approach to the sun, the Parker Solar Probe will reach speeds of 430,000 mph 120
with three main objectives. 124

The first objective of the Parker Solar Probe's mission is to "...trace the flow of 139
energy that heats and accelerates the solar corona and solar wind." The second 152
objective is to "...determine the structure and dynamics of the plasma and 164
magnetic fields at the sources of the solar wind." And third, to "explore 177
mechanisms that accelerate and transport energetic particles." 184

Basically, these objectives will provide new data on solar activity to help us 197
better forecast major space weather events that impact life on earth. We live in 211
the Sun's atmosphere and this mission will help scientists better understand the 223
Sun's impact on Earth. Data from Parker will be key to understanding and 236
forecasting space weather. Space weather can change the orbits of satellites, 247
shorten their lifetimes, or interfere with onboard electronics. 251

The probe is four years into its mission but has a long way to go. 270

Words Read: _____	Words Read: _____	Words Read: _____
minus mistakes: _____	minus mistakes: _____	minus mistakes: _____
equals cwpm: _____	equals cwpm: _____	equals cwpm: _____

Passage 59: Karl Marx

Karl Marx lived from 1818 to 1883. He was a German political philosopher who	14
laid the theory behind the framework for Communism. With his partner and	26
contemporary, Friedrich Engels, Marx wrote the "Communist Manifesto" in 1848	36
seeking to start a Communist revolution around the world. Marx and his theories	49
had tremendous influence over the political and ideological struggles of the	60
twentieth century.	62
Marx believed that Capitalism led to most workers living in poverty while the	75
the nation's wealth was owned by just a few extraordinarily rich capitalists.	87
Marx believed the inequality between the wealthy and the poor was ever-	99
increasing and the working class should overthrow the then current political	110
structure and replace it with a Communist system – a system by which	122
production was owned by the state.	128
Marx believed in a just state and that, in theory…in theory…a Communist	142
system would lead to a just and equal society. Marx did not live to see the	157
Communist revolution and if he had, he would no doubt have been disappointed.	170
The Communism that morphed from Marx's work, when the Soviet Union and	182
China embraced select morsels of his theory, was corrupt and overlooked the	194
essential human rights and equality aspects of his work in their quest for the	208
"dictatorship of the proletariat."	212
Karl Marx's ideals were worthy. He predicted the working class would rise up	225
and it did. He was a philosopher who understood change was necessary to	238
remake life's conditions and the conditions of life during Marx's lifetime were	250
growing poverty and increasing gaps between the wealthy and the workers.	261
He was a humanist, where the victors of the subsequent Communist	272
revolutions were not. Is it therein wherein lies the flaw?	282

Words Read: _____	Words Read: _____	Words Read: _____
minus mistakes: _____	minus mistakes: _____	minus mistakes: _____
equals cwpm: _____	equals cwpm: _____	equals cwpm: _____

Name: _____

Passage 60: Excerpt From Alice's Adventures in Wonderland by Lewis Carroll

Alice was beginning to get very tired of sitting by her sister on the bank, and	16
of having nothing to do: once or twice she had peeped into the book her sister	32
was reading, but it had no pictures or conversations in it, 'and what is the use of	49
a book,' thought Alice 'without pictures or conversation?'	57
So, she was considering in her own mind (as well as she could, for the hot	73
day made her feel very sleepy and stupid), whether the pleasure of making a	87
daisy-chain would be worth the trouble of getting up and picking the daisies,	101
when suddenly a White Rabbit with pink eyes ran close by her.	113
There was nothing so *very* remarkable in that; nor did Alice think it	126
so *very* much out of the way to hear the Rabbit say to itself, 'Oh dear! Oh dear! I	145
shall be late!' (when she thought it over afterwards, it occurred to her that she	160
ought to have wondered at this, but at the time it all seemed quite natural); but	176
when the Rabbit actually *took a watch out of its waistcoat-pocket,* and looked	190
at it, and then hurried on, Alice started to her feet, for it flashed across her mind	207
that she had never before seen a rabbit with either a waistcoat-pocket, or a	222
watch to take out of it, and burning with curiosity, she ran across the field after	238
it, and fortunately was just in time to see it pop down a large rabbit-hole under	256
the hedge.	258
In another moment down went Alice after it, never once considering how in	271
the world she was to get out again.	279
The rabbit-hole went straight on like a tunnel for some way, and then dipped	294
suddenly down, so suddenly that Alice had not a moment to think about	307
stopping herself before she found herself falling.	314

Words Read: _____	Words Read: _____	Words Read: _____
minus mistakes: _____	minus mistakes: _____	minus mistakes: _____
equals cwpm: _____	equals cwpm: _____	equals cwpm: _____

Passage 61: Excerpt From Relativity by Albert Einstein

In your schooldays most of you who read have studied Euclid's geometry,	12
and you remember—perhaps with more respect than love—the teachers who	24
tried to teach it to you. By reason of our past experience, you would certainly	39
regard everyone with disdain who should pronounce this science untrue. But	50
perhaps this feeling of proud certainty would leave you immediately if some	62
one were to ask you: "What, then, do you mean by the assertion that these	77
propositions are true?" Let's give this question a little consideration.	87
Geometry sets out from certain the ideas of "plane," "point," and "straight	99
line," with which we are able to associate more or less definite ideas, and from	114
certain simple propositions which, because of these ideas, we accept as "true."	126
Then, on the basis of a logical process, the justification of which we feel	140
ourselves compelled to admit, all remaining propositions are shown to follow	151
are also proven true.	155
A proposition is then correct ("true") when it has been derived in the	168
recognized manner from another proposition. The question of "truth" of the	179
individual geometrical propositions is reduced to one of the "truth" of the	181
problem. Now it has long been known that the last question is not only	195
unanswerable by the methods of geometry, but that it is in itself entirely	208
without meaning. We cannot ask whether it is true that only one straight line	222
goes through two points. We can only say that Euclidean geometry deals with	235
things called "straight lines," to each of which is ascribed the property of being	249
uniquely determined by two points situated on it. The concept "true" does not	262
tally with the assertions of pure geometry, because by the word "true" we are	276
eventually in the habit of designating always with a "real" object; geometry,	287
however, is not concerned with the relation of the ideas involved when objects	300
are not concrete.	303

Words Read: _____	Words Read: _____	Words Read: _____
minus mistakes: _____	minus mistakes: _____	minus mistakes: _____
equals cwpm: _____	equals cwpm: _____	equals cwpm: _____

Passage 62: The 19th Amendment and Voting Rights

Passed by Congress June 4, 1919, and ratified on August 18, 1920, the 19th	14
amendment granted women the right to vote.	21
The 19th amendment legally guarantees women the right to vote. Achieving	32
this milestone required a lengthy and difficult struggle—victory took decades of	44
agitation and protest. Beginning in the mid-19th century, several generations of	56
woman suffrage supporters lectured, wrote, marched, lobbied, and practiced	65
civil disobedience to achieve what many Americans considered a radical change	76
of the Constitution. Few early supporters lived to see final victory in 1920.	89
Beginning in the 1800s, women organized, petitioned, and picketed to win the	101
right to vote, but it took them decades to accomplish their purpose. Between	114
1878, when the amendment was first introduced in Congress, and August 18,	126
1920, when it was ratified, champions of voting rights for women worked	138
tirelessly, but strategies for achieving their goal varied. Some pursued a	149
strategy of passing suffrage acts in each state—nine western states adopted	161
woman suffrage legislation by 1912. Others challenged male-only voting laws in	173
the courts. Some suffragists used more confrontational tactics such as picketing,	184
silent vigils, and hunger strikes. Often supporters met fierce resistance.	194
Opponents heckled, jailed, and sometimes physically abused them.	202
By 1916, almost all of the major suffrage organizations were united behind the	214
goal of a constitutional amendment. When New York adopted woman suffrage	225
in 1917 and President Wilson changed his position to support an amendment in	238
1918, the political balance began to shift.	245
On May 21, 1919, the House of Representatives passed the amendment, and	257
two weeks later, the Senate followed. When Tennessee became the 36th state to	270
ratify the amendment on August 18, 1920, the amendment passed its final hurdle	283
of obtaining the agreement of three-fourths of the states. The Secretary of State	296
certified the ratification on August 26, 1920, changing the face of the American	309
electorate forever.	311

Words Read: _____	Words Read: _____	Words Read: _____
minus mistakes: _____	minus mistakes: _____	minus mistakes: _____
equals cwpm: _____	equals cwpm: _____	equals cwpm: _____

Passage 63: From George Orwell's Animal Farm

Mr. Jones, of the Manor Farm, had locked the hen-houses for the night, but	15
was too drunk to remember to shut the pop-holes. With the ring of light from his	32
lantern dancing from side to side, he lurched across the yard, kicked off his	46
boots at the back door, drew himself a last glass of beer from the barrel, and	62
made his way up to bed, where Mrs. Jones was already snoring.	74
As soon as the light in the bedroom went out there was a stirring and a	90
fluttering all through the farm buildings. Word had gone round during the day	103
that old Major, the prize Middle White boar, had had a strange dream on the	118
previous night and wished to communicate it to the other animals. It had been	132
agreed that they should all meet in the big barn as soon as Mr. Jones was safely	149
out of the way. Old Major (so he was always called, though the name under	164
which he had been exhibited was Willingdon Beauty) was so highly regarded on	177
the farm that everyone was quite ready to lose an hour's sleep in order to hear	193
what he had to say.	198
At one end of the big barn, on a sort of raised platform, Major was already	213
ensconced on his bed of straw, under a lantern which hung from a beam. He was	229
twelve-years-old and had lately grown rather stout, but he was still a majestic-	244
looking pig, with a wise and benevolent appearance in spite of the fact that his	259
tushes had never been cut. Before long the other animals began to arrive and	273
make themselves comfortable after their different fashions. First came the three	284
dogs, Bluebell, Jessie, and Pincher, and then the pigs, who settled down in the	298
straw immediately in front of the platform. The hens perched themselves on the	309
window-sills, the pigeons fluttered up to the rafters, the sheep and cows lay	223
down behind the pigs and began to chew the cud.	233
All the animals were present except Moses, the tame raven, who slept on a	247
perch behind the back door. When Major saw that they had all made themselves	261
comfortable and were waiting attentively, he cleared his throat and began.	272

Words Read: _____	Words Read: _____	Words Read: _____
minus mistakes: _____	minus mistakes: _____	minus mistakes: _____
equals cwpm: _____	equals cwpm: _____	equals cwpm: _____

Passage 64: What Plants Are

What we commonly call plants, such as corn or buttercups or an oak tree, are | 15

so familiar that a definition of what plants are may seem needless. It would be | 30

quite so if these generally recognized examples comprised all the plant | 41

kingdom. Actually, what are ordinarily thought of as plants make up only a | 54

fraction of the great plant world. The fact that our familiar roadside and garden | 68

plants produce blossoms followed by a fruit and seed, such as peas and beans | 82

and all the ordinary flora of any region, separates them at once from that other | 97

large group of plants that do not. | 104

Common examples of the latter class are the green scum on the ponds, moss, | 118

seaweed, the rust on wheat, yeast, disease-causing bacteria, the smallest of all | 131

known plants, and many others. Most of these organisms are so small that they | 145

can be distinguished only under the higher powers of the microscope. Some of | 158

them in their habits and growth are like the minute animals described in the | 172

volume of this series devoted to that subject. In fact, there are organisms about | 186

which scientists are still in doubt as to their animal or vegetable character. | 199

One or two characteristics common to most plants, however, separate them | 210

from animals and these are their method of getting food and their | 221

practically immovable mode of life. Animals, however simple, do eat and digest | 233

their food, plants take various mineral substances from the earth or air or water | 246

in the form of inorganic matter such as oxygen, carbon, nitrogen, and all the | 260

food materials found in the soil, and transform them, with the aid of sunshine, | 274

into the structure that characterizes each particular form. Plants, then, may be | 286

defined as any living organism that, with minor exceptions, has the power to | 299

assimilate inorganic substances and transform them into organic | 307

matter. Nothing else in all the realm of nature has this power. | 319

Words Read: _____	Words Read: _____	Words Read: _____
minus mistakes: _____	minus mistakes: _____	minus mistakes: _____
equals cwpm: _____	equals cwpm: _____	equals cwpm: _____

Name: _____

Passage 65: The Gettysburg Address

This is the Bliss copy of President Lincoln's famous Gettysburg Address. It is	13
the most often reproduced and the copy on display in the Lincoln Room at the	28
White House. It was recopied by Lincoln and given to Colonel Alexander Bliss to	42
use as a fundraiser for soldiers.	48
Four score and seven years ago our fathers brought forth on this continent, a	62
new nation, conceived in Liberty, and dedicated to the proposition that all men	75
are created equal.	78
Now we are engaged in a great civil war, testing whether that nation, or any	93
nation so conceived and so dedicated, can long endure. We are met on a great	108
battlefield of that war. We have come to dedicate a portion of that field, as a	125
final resting place for those who here gave their lives that that nation might live.	141
It is altogether fitting and proper that we should do this.	152
But, in a larger sense, we can not dedicate -- we can not consecrate -- we can	167
not hallow -- this ground. The brave men, living and dead, who struggled here,	170
have consecrated it, far above our poor power to add or detract. The world will	185
little note, nor long remember what we say here, but it can never forget what	200
they did here. It is for us the living, rather, to be dedicated here to the	216
unfinished work which they who fought here have thus far so nobly advanced. It	230
is rather for us to be here dedicated to the great task remaining before us --	245
that from these honored dead we take increased devotion to that cause for	258
which they gave the last full measure of devotion -- that we here highly resolve	272
that these dead shall not have died in vain -- that this nation, under God, shall	287
have a new birth of freedom -- and that government of the people, by the	301
people, for the people, shall not perish from the earth.	311
Abraham Lincoln	313
November 19, 1863	316

Words Read: _____	Words Read: _____	Words Read: _____
minus mistakes: _____	minus mistakes: _____	minus mistakes: _____
equals cwpm: _____	equals cwpm: _____	equals cwpm: _____

Passage 66: Yosemite

The valleys, waterfalls, meadows, granite cliffs, and glaciers of Yosemite	13
National Park are nestled in the Sierra Nevada Mountains in Central California.	28
Ever majestic, and ever-changing, the landscape of Yosemite is not what it was	42
450 million years ago. Uplift, erosion, and glaciation have shaped the scenery	48
into what is the grandeur of the park today.	62
Since 2.6 million years ago there have been more than 40 cycles of glacial	75
(cold) and interglacial (warm) periods. These glacial periods modified the	78
landscape forming Yosemite Valley, other canyons, lakes, and many of the other	93
features seen in Yosemite today.	108
Yosemite was designated a World Heritage Site in 1984, and is internationally	125
recognized for its granite cliffs, clear streams, waterfalls, giant sequoia groves,	141
lakes, meadows, mountains, and glaciers. Approximately 95% of the park is	152
designated wilderness.	167
Yosemite is 1,189 square miles which is about the same size as Rhode Island.	170
It contains 1000s of lakes, over 1,600 miles of streams, 800 miles of hiking trails,	185
and 350 roads. An average of 4 million people visit the park annually with most	200
staying in the seven-square miles known as Yosemite Valley.	216
Popular sights at Yosemite include Yosemite Falls, Half Dome, Glacier Point, El	230
Capitan, Yosemite Valley, Tunnel View, Nevada Falls and the giant groves of	245
sequoias.	258
Yosemite was instrumental in the establishment of the national park idea	272
when Galen Clark and others lobbied to protect it from development. This led to	287
President Abraham Lincoln signing the Yosemite Grant of 1864. Then in 1890,	301
John Muir petitioned to Congress to establish it as the nation's third national	311
park. They did.	313
	316

Words Read: _____	Words Read: _____	Words Read: _____
minus mistakes: _____	minus mistakes: _____	minus mistakes: _____
equals cwpm: _____	equals cwpm: _____	equals cwpm: _____

Passage 67: Kobe Bryant 2

Kobe Bryant was an American professional basketball player dubbed one of	11
the greatest players of all time. In 1996, the shooting guard, who spent his entire	26
career with the Los Angeles Lakers, became one of the of select few to enter the	42
NBA draft directly out of high school. The extraordinarily gifted shooting guard	54
was ranked the 13th overall draft pick at 18-years-old.	65
Kobe was a high-flyer and a fan favorite who, in 2004, became the	80
cornerstone of the Los Angeles Lakers. He led the NBA in scoring during 2005-06	95
and 2006-07 seasons which earned him the honor of the National Basketball	107
Association MVP title in 2008. His all-time career high score of 81 points in a	124
single game was achieved in 2006; it is the second most points scored in any one	139
game behind Wilt Chamberlain's 100 points in 1962.	146
Kobe was the first guard in NBA history to play 20 seasons, his 18 All-Star	162
designations is a league second, and he is the only NBA player to have multiple	177
numbers retired by the same franchise. They are Nos. 8 and 24 with the Lakers.	192
Kobe's won 5 NBA championships and was the NBA Finals MVP two times, the All-	206
Star game MVP four times, and made the All-NBA First Team 11 times.	221
Kobe brought his high-flying feats to the Olympic games in 2008 and 2012	235
when he helped team USA win two gold medals. The basketball great retired after	248
the 2015-16 seasons when he was plagued by knee and shoulder injuries.	261
Kobe met his tragic death in 2020 when he, his daughter, and seven others	275
died in a helicopter accident in Southern California. Numerous accolades followed	285
– including naming the All-Star MVP Award in his honor.	296

Words Read:	Words Read:	Words Read:
minus mistakes:	minus mistakes:	minus mistakes:
equals cwpm:	equals cwpm:	equals cwpm:

Passage 68: Elle Fanning

Elle Fanning is an American actress best known for portraying Aurora in the | 13
Maleficent film series. Elle's been acting a long time - making her film debut | 26
playing the younger version of her sister – Dakota Fanning - in the movie *I Am* | 40
Sam. | 41

Elle is a Hollywood powerhouse, making eight films in five years. The young | 54
thespian favors independent films and has graced the screen in *Teen Spirit* and *I* | 68
Think We Are Alone Now. At only 21, Elle has made over 40 films and was the | 85
youngest judge in history at the Cannes Film Festival. | 94

Elle was born in Georgia to a professional tennis player and minor league | 107
baseball player. With athletics in her genes, Elle loves playing soccer and | 119
volleyball. She also likes to draw and lounge around with her sister. They enjoy | 133
watching the show *Fear Factor and* riding their horses. | 142

Elle is a superstar who is known to be down-to-earth. She may be a movie | 159
star, but she likes to do normal things with her family best of all. | 173

Elle's favorite role was playing Empress Catherine II in the Hulu series *The* | 186
Great, for which she received a Primetime Emmy Award for Outstanding Lead | 198
Actress in a Comedy Series nomination as well as two Golden Globe | 210
Award nominations and three Screen Actors Guild Award nominations. In 2022, | 221
she starred as Michelle Carter in the Hulu limited series *The Girl from Plainville*. | 235

Words Read:	Words Read:	Words Read:
minus mistakes:	minus mistakes:	minus mistakes:
equals cwpm:	equals cwpm:	equals cwpm:

Passage 69: Gal Gadot

Gal Gadot is the current "it girl" of the silver screen. The Israeli actress, | 14

producer, model and director is an unstoppable force that has taken Hollywood | 26

by storm. | 28

Gadot was born in Tel Aviv, Israel, and is the grandchild of Holocaust | 41

survivors. | 42

Gadot shot to stardom playing Diana Prince, AKA Wonder Woman, in the DC | 55

Extended Universe films *Batman vs. Superman: Dawn of Justice* (2016), *Wonder* | 66

Woman (2017), and *Justice League* (2017). | 72

At age 18, Gadot entered the national Miss Israel beauty pageant never | 84

thinking she'd win, but she did and subsequently competed in the Miss Universe | 97

Pageant in Ecuador. At age 20, she enlisted in the Israel Defense Forces as a | 112

combat fitness instructor as part of her mandatory two years of Israeli military | 125

service. Of her time in the service, Gadot says "You give two or three years, and | 141

it's not about you. You give your freedom away for a while for the freedom of | 157

everyone." | 158

From there, Gadot studied law at IDC Herzliya in Israel. In 2013, Gadot was | 172

ranked as the second highest earning fashion model in Israel and one of the | 186

faces of Gucci, Revlon and Reebok. | 192

Now, her acting career is off and running. We can expect big things from her! | 207

Words Read:	Words Read:	Words Read:
minus mistakes:	minus mistakes:	minus mistakes:
equals cwpm:	equals cwpm:	equals cwpm:

Name: _____

Passage 70: Carissa Moore – Champion of the Waves

Carissa Moore's journey to becoming one of the world's most accomplished	11
surfers is as inspiring as it is impressive. Born in Honolulu, Hawaii, Carissa was	25
introduced to surfing at a young age by her father, who nurtured her love for the	41
ocean and the sport. She quickly rose through the ranks, joining the World Surf	55
League (WSL) Championship Tour in 2010 when she was only 18. Her drive,	68
dedication, and raw talent led her to claim her first WSL Championship title in	82
2011, marking the beginning of a historic career. Over the years, she continued to	96
dominate the sport, winning five WSL Championship titles in 2011, 2013, 2015,	108
2019, and 2021, showcasing her ability to stay at the top of her game even as the	125
competition grew stronger.	127
In 2014, Carissa's achievements were recognized with her induction into the	138
Surfers' Hall of Fame, a rare honor that celebrated her impact on the sport. Her	153
success reached new heights at the Tokyo 2020 Olympics, where she won the	166
first-ever Olympic gold medal in women's shortboard surfing, a monumental	177
achievement that cemented her legacy and inspired surfers around the world.	189
Carissa's journey has not been without challenges, but her perseverance and	200
positive outlook have made her a beloved figure in the surfing community.	212
Carissa Moore is more than a world champion; she's a role model for aspiring	226
athletes. Her commitment to sportsmanship, humility, and passion for surfing	236
have set her apart as a true icon. By breaking records and paving the way for	252
future generations of female surfers, Carissa has shown that with hard work,	264
resilience, and a love for the ocean, anyone can reach the heights of success. Her	279
legacy will undoubtedly inspire surfers for years to come.	288

Words Read:	Words Read:	Words Read:
minus mistakes:	minus mistakes:	minus mistakes:
equals cwpm:	equals cwpm:	equals cwpm:

Name: _____

Passage 71: Alex Morgan – Soccer Trailblazer

Alex Morgan's impact on the world of women's soccer goes far beyond her	13
accomplishments on the field. Known for her speed, skill, and fierce determination, Alex	26
quickly rose to prominence as a vital member of the U.S. Women's National Team	40
(USWNT). Her journey began in earnest in 2012 when, at just 22 years old, she became	56
the sixth and youngest American player to score 20 goals in a single season. That same	72
year, she made an unforgettable impact at the London Olympics, scoring a game-	85
winning goal in the semifinal against Canada that propelled the U.S. team to the gold	100
medal match.	102
Alex's career continued to flourish as she played an instrumental role in the USWNT's	116
victories at the 2015 and 2019 FIFA Women's World Cups. Her outstanding performance	129
in 2019 earned her the Silver Boot, a prestigious honor awarded to one of the	144
tournament's top scorers. Throughout her career, Alex has been a vocal advocate for	157
equal pay and better conditions for female athletes, using her platform to bring attention	171
to the gender disparities in sports.	177
Beyond her athletic prowess, Alex Morgan is a role model for young athletes and an	192
advocate for gender equality in sports. Her dedication to excellence, both on and off the	207
field, has inspired countless girls to pursue their dreams in soccer and beyond. Alex's	221
influence extends far beyond the pitch; she's a trailblazer who has fought for fairness,	235
recognition, and respect for female athletes. Her legacy is one of resilience, leadership,	248
and an unwavering commitment to making the world of sports a better place for future	263
generations.	264

Words Read:	Words Read:	Words Read:
minus mistakes:	minus mistakes:	minus mistakes:
equals cwpm:	equals cwpm:	equals cwpm:

Passage 72: Dalilah Muhammad Hurdler

Dalilah Muhammad's journey in track and field is a story of perseverance,	12
speed, and breaking barriers. Born in Queens, New York, Dalilah developed a	24
passion for running at a young age. Her specialty, the 400-meter hurdles, would	38
ultimately become the event where she made history. Dalilah's talent was evident	50
early in her career, as she quickly rose through the ranks of American track and	65
field, earning silver medals in the 400-meter hurdles at the World Championships	78
in 2013 and 2017. However, her defining moment came in 2019, when she set a	93
world record with a time of 52.16 seconds at the World Championships, becoming	106
the first woman in history to break that barrier.	115
Her accomplishment was the result of years of intense training, resilience, and	127
an unbreakable focus on her goals. Dalilah's world record did not come easily; she	141
had to overcome numerous setbacks and challenges, including injuries and the	152
fierce competition of her event. Yet, her determination and mental strength	163
allowed her to push through, culminating in one of the most celebrated	175
performances in track and field history.	181
Dalilah Muhammad's success has made her a role model for young athletes,	193
particularly girls who aspire to compete at the highest levels of their sport. She	207
embodies the spirit of resilience and the power of perseverance, showing that	219
success is achievable with hard work and dedication. By breaking records and	231
shattering expectations, Dalilah has redefined what is possible in women's track	242
and field, inspiring a new generation of athletes to chase their dreams and	255
believe in their potential.	259

Words Read:	Words Read:	Words Read:
minus mistakes:	minus mistakes:	minus mistakes:
equals cwpm:	equals cwpm:	equals cwpm:

Passage 73: Mackenzie Ziegler – Fact and Opinion

Mackenzie Ziegler, born on June 4, 2004, began her music career in 2014 with	14
her debut album, *Mack Z*. Following its success, she released her second studio	27
album, *Phases*, in 2018. Since then, Ziegler has collaborated with singer Johnny	39
Orlando on multiple projects, including joint concert tours across North America	50
and Europe. She and Orlando have released several singles together, and Ziegler	62
has also launched numerous solo releases, building a strong fan base with her	75
music. In addition to her music career, she has modeled for major brands like	89
Polo Ralph Lauren, a venture that has become an important part of her	102
professional life.	104
Ziegler first gained fame on the reality show *Dance Moms*, but her TV	117
appearances have extended beyond dance. She has guest-starred on shows like	129
Nicky, Ricky, Dicky & Dawn (2015 and 2017) and starred in the high school drama	143
Total Eclipse on Brat TV from 2018 to 2020. Her performance talents took her to	158
the stage in 2018, when she competed *on Dancing with the Stars: Juniors* and	172
starred as Dorothy in the holiday pantomime *The Wonderful Winter of Oz* in	185
Pasadena, California.	187
By 2024, Ziegler's social media following has grown significantly. She has over	199
15 million followers on Instagram, around 24 million on TikTok, more than 3.5	212
million YouTube subscribers, and 1.2 million Twitter followers. Her continued	222
success across music, television, and social media demonstrates her versatility	232
and growing influence in the entertainment industry.	239

Words Read:	Words Read:	Words Read:
minus mistakes:	minus mistakes:	minus mistakes:
equals cwpm:	equals cwpm:	equals cwpm:

Passage 74: The History of Hershey

The history of Hershey chocolate begins with its founder, Milton S. Hershey, a | 13
visionary entrepreneur with a passion for making quality chocolate accessible to | 24
the masses. Born in 1857 in Pennsylvania, Hershey initially pursued careers in | 36
caramel-making and candy production. After several setbacks and failed | 46
business ventures, Hershey finally found success with the Lancaster Caramel | 56
Company, which he sold for a significant sum in 1900. This sale allowed him to | 71
turn his attention fully to chocolate, a growing trend he had witnessed at the | 85
World's Columbian Exposition in Chicago in 1893. | 92

Hershey's ultimate goal was to create affordable, high-quality milk chocolate, | 103
a product previously reserved for the wealthy. In 1903, he began building the | 116
world's largest chocolate manufacturing plant in Derry Township, Pennsylvania. | 125
Using fresh milk from local dairy farms, Hershey developed a unique, creamy milk | 138
chocolate that was delicious yet inexpensive to produce. By 1905, Hershey's | 149
factory was operational, and his chocolate bars quickly became popular across | 160
the United States. | 163

Hershey's success wasn't just in his chocolate; he also founded the town of | 176
Hershey, Pennsylvania, a place for his employees to live with amenities like | 188
schools, parks, and recreational facilities. This model community helped attract a | 199
loyal workforce. Today, Hershey's legacy endures through The Hershey Company, | 209
which continues to innovate and expand, solidifying Hershey's reputation as "The | 220
Great American Chocolate Bar." The Hershey brand remains iconic worldwide, | 230
symbolizing quality, affordability, and the sweet success of a man who believed | 242
in making chocolate for everyone. | 247

Words Read:	Words Read:	Words Read:
minus mistakes:	minus mistakes:	minus mistakes:
equals cwpm:	equals cwpm:	equals cwpm:

Passage 75: Jack Dylan Grazer

Jack Dylan Grazer is an American actor known for his roles in both film and	15
television, capturing attention with his talent, charisma, and maturity in handling	26
diverse roles. Born on September 3, 2003, in Los Angeles, California, Grazer was	39
exposed to the entertainment industry early on, and he demonstrated a strong	51
passion for acting from a young age. His breakout role came in 2017 when he	66
starred as Eddie Kaspbrak in the film adaptation of Stephen King's *It*, where his	80
portrayal of the hypochondriac, witty, and loyal Eddie garnered significant praise	91
from audiences and critics alike. Grazer's performance helped elevate the horror	102
movie into a mainstream success, marking him as a rising talent in Hollywood.	115
Following *It*, Grazer continued to impress with his versatility, taking on the role	128
of Freddy Freeman in the 2019 superhero film *Shazam!*, where he brought humor	141
and depth to the character. His portrayal offered a fresh, relatable perspective	153
on the superhero genre, earning him accolades and further expanding his fan	165
base. Grazer's career reflects not only his acting skills but also his dedication to	179
authentic storytelling, as he consistently chooses roles that challenge and inspire	190
him. Off-screen, Grazer has been vocal about issues like mental health, openly	203
discussing his own experiences and encouraging others to be resilient and seek	215
support.	216

Words Read:	Words Read:	Words Read:
minus mistakes:	minus mistakes:	minus mistakes:
equals cwpm:	equals cwpm:	equals cwpm:

Passage 76: Bradley Cooper

Bradley Cooper is a versatile American actor and filmmaker known for his	12
transformative performances and his dedication to complex, challenging roles.	21
Born on January 5, 1975, in Philadelphia, Pennsylvania, Cooper pursued a career	33
in the arts with a degree in English from Georgetown University before studying	46
at the Actors Studio Drama School in New York City. His breakthrough role came	60
with the 2009 comedy *The Hangover*, where his portrayal of Phil, the charming,	73
slightly irreverent leader of a group of friends, made him a household name and	87
showcased his knack for both humor and wit.	95

However, Cooper's career soon evolved beyond comedy as he took on diverse,	107
intense roles in dramas and thrillers. His performance as Pat Solitano, a man	120
grappling with mental illness in *Silver Linings Playbook* (2012), earned him his first	133
Academy Award nomination, and he later received critical acclaim for his roles in	146
American Sniper (2014) and *American Hustle* (2013).	153

In 2018, Cooper directed, co-wrote, and starred in *A Star is Born*, a passion	168
project that demonstrated his multifaceted talents and earned him multiple	178
award nominations. Beyond his talent, Cooper is admired for his commitment to	190
authenticity, often immersing himself in rigorous training and research for his	201
roles. Known for his grounded personality, Bradley Cooper remains one of	212
Hollywood's most respected and influential actors, balancing mainstream appeal	221
with powerful performances that resonate deeply with audiences.	229

Words Read:	Words Read:	Words Read:
minus mistakes:	minus mistakes:	minus mistakes:
equals cwpm:	equals cwpm:	equals cwpm:

Passage 77: Six Flags

Six Flags stands as one of the world's premier amusement park chains, with	13
roots tracing back to 1961. Founded by Angus G. Wynne in Arlington, Texas, the	27
first park, Six Flags Over Texas, was designed to celebrate the state's diverse	40
heritage. Its name honors the six flags of the nations that once ruled over Texas.	55
The park quickly gained popularity, featuring attractions and rides themed	65
around these historical influences. Seeing its success, Six Flags began expanding	76
in the 1970s, adding locations in Georgia and Missouri and gradually acquiring	88
other parks across the U.S. By the 1990s, Six Flags had firmly established itself	103
with parks in major cities nationwide, introducing cutting-edge roller coasters	114
and water rides that drew thrill-seekers from all around.	124
In addition to thrilling rides, the company's partnership with Warner Bros.	135
allowed it to feature Looney Tunes characters and DC Comics superheroes,	146
boosting appeal for families and younger visitors alike. Despite its growing	157
success, Six Flags faced significant financial difficulties in the early 2000s,	168
leading to a bankruptcy filing in 2009. However, the company soon restructured	180
and refocused, emerging stronger and committed to enhancing its park	190
experiences.	191
Today, Six Flags operates numerous parks throughout North America,	200
continuing to captivate visitors with innovative rides and themed seasonal	210
events. Known for its iconic roller coasters and immersive attractions, Six Flags	220
remains a leader in the theme park industry.	230

Words Read:	Words Read:	Words Read:
minus mistakes:	minus mistakes:	minus mistakes:
equals cwpm:	equals cwpm:	equals cwpm:

Reading 78: Frequency Word List 1200

abrasive	abruptly	acknowledge	acquire	addict	5
adequate	allege	alternative	amendment	attribute	10
authentic	bewilderment	bias	boycott	candor	15
cause	compel	competent	concur	condemn	20
confront	consult	correspond	deceit	demeanor	25
devastate	devour	diversity	eligible	emphasize	20
estimate	evaluate	famished	harass	impartial	35
indifferent	initiate	intimidate	legendary	mandatory	40
mitigate	narrate	necessity	negligent	omit	45
opposition	oppress	perceive	prediction	prominent	50
punctual	quote	relinquish	resolve	rudimentary	55
succession	sovereign	suspense	toxic	viewpoint	60
unity	agility	humidity	honesty	specialty	65
safety	amnesty	agreement	payment	treatment	70
civic	volcanic	magnetic	heroic	fabulous	75
numerous	vigorous	monstrous	informative	conservative	80
complete	conditions	credible	impartial	cynic	85
reconcile	redundant	pacify	flatter	formulate	90
punitive	abrupt	adopt	adorn	abstract	95
awkward	arena	attend	facet	extreme	100

Words Read: _____	Words Read: _____	Words Read: _____
minus mistakes: _____	minus mistakes: _____	minus mistakes: _____
equals cwpm: _____	equals cwpm: _____	equals cwpm: _____

Name: _____

Passage 79: Frequency Word Level 1300

criticism	critically	depict	contemporary	increasingly	5
conference	induce	primarily	existence	devote	10
twentieth	retain	innovation	compel	dramatically	15
influential	sustain	elsewhere	nevertheless	capable	20
absence	moderate	marginal	perception	isolation	25
extensive	lifestyle	productive	distinctive	consumption	20
frequent	refine	distinction	merge	uncertainty	35
formulate	discipline	motivate	consideration	readily	40
sharply	initially	descent	disrupt	disperse	45
evident	abundance	regain	tremendous	induction	50
devise	paradox	phenomenon	acknowledge	implement	55
administer	necessity	ongoing	costly	transitional	60
renew	indirectly	differentiate	inferior	beneficial	65
intermediate	notion	tolerance	defect	incidence	70
patent	contradict	manual	cooperative	repeatedly	75
unequal	comprise	enrich	instruct	attain	80
diverge	designate	distort	profession	completion	85
permanently	plentiful	consequently	constitute	dependence	90
resistant	dominance	acceptance	adjustment	framework	95
undermine	validity	voluntary	deliberate	successive	100

Words Read: _____
minus mistakes: _____
equals cwpm: _____

Words Read: _____
minus mistakes: _____
equals cwpm: _____

Words Read: _____
minus mistakes: _____
equals cwpm: _____

Passage 80: Frequency Word Level List 1400

precaution	dilemma	merit	therapy	latter	5
nutrition	embody	abruptly	collaborative	consistently	10
lowering	overview	uneven	unlikely	colleague	15
credible	notable	outward	inward	intrigue	20
explicitly	fallacy	recur	deficiency	drawback	25
contradictory	duration	refute	copyright	discard	20
faulty	hereditary	inexpensive	loosely	respective	35
wane	concise	predictable	prominence	simplicity	40
sympathetic	withstand	appropriately	exclusion	abbreviate	45
enjoyment	prescribe	deem	diagnose	periodically	50
innovative	minimal	neatly	intricate	premise	55
prevention	readiness	affordable	discern	dissimilar	60
implication	unclear	additionally	innate	likelihood	65
peculiar	speculation	chiefly	conform	indefinitely	70
orally	reliability	usable	elapse	mainstream	75
noticeable	nuance	outweigh	progression	setback	80
counterpart	discourse	inaccurate	misuse	satisfy	85
dual	excel	heed	recede	assertion	90
annotation	esteem	inefficient	lifelong	forceful	95
optimistic	uncontrolled	vividly	locally	wasteful	100

Words Read: _____ minus mistakes: _____ equals cwpm: _____	Words Read: _____ minus mistakes: _____ equals cwpm: _____	Words Read: _____ minus mistakes: _____ equals cwpm: _____

Set 5: 1050L-1300L

Note: These passages range from 1050L-1300L and are intended to be used in order. They are purposely in this high school range and not individually leveled because they represent a research-based span that helps prepare students for reading beyond high school.

Some of the fiction passages have a repeated sentence from the end of one to the beginning of another. This is intentional so each can function as a stand-alone reading passage and make sense to the reader.

Passage 81: The Inspiration Behind Snow White

The story of the real Snow White is believed to be inspired by the life of a	17
young girl named Margaretha von Waldeck, who lived in Germany during the	29
16th century. Born in 1533, Margaretha was the daughter of Philip IV, a count who	44
ruled over a mining town called Waldeck. Her life shared many elements with the	58
famous fairy tale, though the real story was darker and more tragic.	70
Margaretha's father owned copper mines where young children were used for	81
labor. These children worked in difficult, dangerous conditions and were often	92
underfed, leading to stunted growth. As a result, they looked much smaller than	105
other children, which may have inspired the "seven dwarfs" who lived in the	118
forest in Snow White.	122
When Margaretha was a teenager, she was sent away to the royal court in	136
Brussels. Known for her beauty, she caught the attention of many noblemen,	148
including Prince Philip II of Spain. However, this attracted jealousy and	159
resentment from powerful people at court. It's believed that Margaretha's beauty	170
and connections made her a target for poisoning, likely ordered by people who	183
saw her as a threat to their power.	191
Margaretha died at just 21 under mysterious circumstances. Many historians	201
believe she was poisoned, echoing the poisoned apple from the fairy tale. Her	214
story spread over the years, and elements of her life were likely adapted and	228
softened into the Snow White we know today.	236
The Brothers Grimm collected German folklore and included Snow White in	247
their famous fairy tale collection. Over time, the story evolved, but some	259
historians believe the tragic life of Margaretha von Waldeck left an impression on	272
the world, transforming her into a legendary figure that would live on in the	286
timeless tale of Snow White.	291

Words Read:	Words Read:	Words Read:
minus mistakes:	minus mistakes:	minus mistakes:
equals cwpm:	equals cwpm:	equals cwpm:

Passage 82: The Inspiration for Frozen

The Disney movie *Frozen* was inspired by the fairy tale *The Snow Queen*,	13
written by Danish author Hans Christian Andersen in 1844. However, the original	25
story and characters are quite different from Disney's adaptation.	34
In *The Snow Queen*, the story follows two children, Gerda and Kai, who are	48
best friends. One day, Kai gets a shard of a magical, evil mirror stuck in his heart	65
and eye, causing him to become cold and mean. *The Snow Queen*, a powerful, icy	80
figure, takes him to her frozen palace far in the north. Gerda, heartbroken by her	95
friend's disappearance, sets off on a dangerous journey to find and rescue him.	108
Along the way, she encounters many magical creatures and faces difficult	119
challenges. Eventually, her love and kindness melt the shard in Kai's heart, freeing	132
him from the Snow Queen's spell.	138
The original Snow Queen character is different from Elsa, the heroine of	150
Frozen. In Andersen's tale, the Snow Queen is a mysterious, distant figure, almost	163
like a villain, while Elsa is portrayed as a misunderstood character struggling with	176
her powers. Disney transformed the character of the Snow Queen into Elsa, a	189
young woman with magical ice powers who feels isolated due to her abilities.	202
Disney's *Frozen* kept the themes of love and bravery but turned the focus onto	216
family bonds, particularly between sisters Elsa and Anna. Unlike Andersen's story,	227
where the main friendship is between two childhood friends, *Frozen* centers on	239
Anna's love for her sister Elsa and her determination to bring her back from	253
isolation.	254
Though *Frozen* took significant creative liberties, it still drew inspiration from	265
Andersen's themes of love overcoming darkness. The tale of *The Snow Queen*	277
continues to resonate, adapted into a story that celebrates the power of family,	290
courage, and self-acceptance.	294

Words Read:	Words Read:	Words Read:
minus mistakes:	minus mistakes:	minus mistakes:
equals cwpm:	equals cwpm:	equals cwpm:

Name: _____

Passage 83: Patrick Mahomes

Patrick Mahomes is one of the most exciting players in professional football	12
today. Born in 1995 in Tyler, Texas, Mahomes grew up with a passion for sports.	27
His father, Pat Mahomes, was a professional baseball player, which exposed	38
Patrick to athletics from a young age. Although he excelled in baseball, Mahomes	51
found his true calling in football. In high school, he played both football and	65
baseball, earning recognition for his impressive skills as a quarterback.	75
Mahomes attended Texas Tech University, where he set records with his	86
powerful arm and ability to make difficult throws. In 2017, he entered the NFL	100
Draft and was selected by the Kansas City Chiefs in the first round. By his second	116
season, Mahomes had taken the league by storm. In 2018, he became the starting	130
quarterback for the Chiefs and amazed fans with his incredible passing ability,	142
leading the team to a 12-4 record. That year, he threw for over 5,000 yards and	158
50 touchdowns, winning the NFL MVP award.	165
In 2020, Mahomes led the Chiefs to their first Super Bowl win in 50 years,	170
defeating the San Francisco 49ers. His performance earned him the Super Bowl	182
MVP title, solidifying his reputation as one of the league's best. Known for his	196
athleticism, Mahomes can make throws from various angles, often surprising	206
defenses. His signature no-look passes and deep throws have become his	218
trademark, making him a unique talent in the NFL.	227
Off the field, Mahomes is involved in charitable work and supports causes in his	241
community. He started the "15 and the Mahomies" foundation to help children	253
through health, education, and community programs. Today, Patrick Mahomes	262
continues to inspire fans and young athletes, proving that hard work and talent	275
can lead to extraordinary achievements.	280

Words Read:	Words Read:	Words Read:
minus mistakes:	minus mistakes:	minus mistakes:
equals cwpm:	equals cwpm:	equals cwpm:

Passage 84: A'ja Wilson

A'ja Wilson is a standout athlete and one of the most talented players in	14
women's basketball. Born in Hopkins, South Carolina, in 1996, Wilson grew up in a	28
family that loved sports. Her father was a professional basketball player	39
overseas, which inspired her love for the game. She began playing basketball at a	53
young age and quickly excelled, becoming a star player in high school. Wilson	66
attended Heathwood Hall Episcopal School, where she set multiple records and	77
gained attention as one of the top high school players in the country.	90
After high school, Wilson chose to attend the University of South Carolina.	102
There, she played under legendary coach Dawn Staley and led her team to the	116
NCAA Championship in 2017, where they won the title. During her college career,	129
Wilson's performance on the court was unmatched, and she became a three-time	142
SEC Player of the Year and a unanimous First-Team All-American. In 2018, she	157
won the Naismith College Player of the Year award, recognizing her as the best	171
player in women's college basketball.	176
After her successful college career, Wilson was the first overall pick in the 2018	190
WNBA Draft, selected by the Las Vegas Aces. She made an immediate impact in	204
the WNBA, winning Rookie of the Year. In 2020, she led the Aces to the WNBA	220
Finals and won the league MVP award. Known for her scoring ability, defensive	233
skills, and leadership, Wilson has become one of the most respected players in the	247
league.	248
Beyond basketball, Wilson is passionate about giving back. She created the	259
A'ja Wilson Foundation to raise awareness for dyslexia, a learning disorder she	271
personally experienced. Through her foundation, she supports programs that help	281
children with learning disabilities. A'ja Wilson's talent, hard work, and dedication	292
to her community make her an inspiring figure both on and off the court.	306

Words Read:	Words Read:	Words Read:
minus mistakes:	minus mistakes:	minus mistakes:
equals cwpm:	equals cwpm:	equals cwpm:

Passage 85: Donna Langley

Donna Langley is a leading figure in the entertainment industry, known for her | 13
work as the Chairwoman of Universal Pictures. Born in England, Langley began | 25
her career in film in the 1990s, working her way up through various roles in | 40
Hollywood. Her journey from a junior position to one of the most powerful | 53
executives in the industry reflects her dedication, vision, and understanding of | 64
the movie business. | 67

Langley joined Universal Pictures in 2001 and quickly made a name for herself | 80
as a strong and innovative leader. Over the years, she has overseen the | 92
production of numerous successful films, bringing fresh ideas to the company and | 104
helping to shape the future of Hollywood. Under her leadership, Universal | 115
produced major franchises like *Jurassic World, Fast & Furious*, and *Despicable* | 125
Me, which have all become global hits. Her approach blends blockbuster | 136
entertainment with diverse storytelling, creating a slate of films that appeals to | 148
audiences around the world. | 152

One of Langley's major accomplishments has been her support for diverse and | 164
inclusive stories. She has championed films with strong female leads, like *Pitch* | 176
Perfect and *Fifty Shades of Grey*, and has been a key figure in bringing stories | 191
with different cultural perspectives to the screen. Langley is known for taking | 203
risks on unique projects, such as *Get Out*, which became a cultural phenomenon | 216
and earned critical acclaim. | 220

Langley's influence extends beyond film production; she has also been | 230
instrumental in navigating changes in the industry, including the shift toward | 241
streaming and digital releases. As one of the few women in a top studio executive | 256
role, Langley is a trailblazer who continues to inspire others in Hollywood. Her | 259
impact on Universal Pictures and the industry as a whole demonstrates her | 271
commitment to evolving storytelling and creating films that resonate with a | 282
global audience. | 284

Words Read:	Words Read:	Words Read:
minus mistakes:	minus mistakes:	minus mistakes:
equals cwpm:	equals cwpm:	equals cwpm:

Passage 86: Jim Thorpe

Jim Thorpe is considered one of the greatest athletes in American history, | 12

excelling in multiple sports and leaving a lasting legacy in athletics. Born in 1887 | 26

in what is now Oklahoma, Thorpe was a member of the Sac and Fox Nation and | 42

grew up in a challenging environment, facing the hardships of Native American | 54

discrimination. Despite these obstacles, Thorpe developed exceptional athletic | 62

skills from a young age. | 67

Thorpe attended the Carlisle Indian Industrial School in Pennsylvania, where | 77

he played multiple sports under the legendary coach Pop Warner. It was here | 90

that Thorpe's talent truly began to shine. In 1912, he competed in the Stockholm | 104

Olympics, where he won gold medals in both the pentathlon and decathlon, | 116

events that required a wide range of athletic abilities. His remarkable | 127

performance amazed spectators, and he was celebrated as one of the best | 139

athletes in the world. However, due to controversy over his past participation in | 152

minor league baseball, Thorpe was stripped of his Olympic medals—a decision | 164

that was only reversed in 1983, long after his death. | 174

Beyond the Olympics, Thorpe had an impressive career in professional sports. | 185

He played baseball for the New York Giants and the Cincinnati Reds and was also | 200

one of the pioneers of professional football. Thorpe played in the National | 212

Football League (NFL) and became the first president of what would later | 124

become the NFL. His strength, speed, and versatility set a standard for future | 137

athletes. | 138

Thorpe's legacy goes beyond his athletic achievements. He broke racial | 148

barriers and became an inspiration for Native Americans and athletes around the | 160

world. His life story reflects both triumph and hardship, and his achievements | 172

continue to be celebrated. Today, Jim Thorpe is remembered not only as an | 185

exceptional athlete but also as a symbol of resilience and dedication in sports | 198

history. | 199

Words Read:	Words Read:	Words Read:
minus mistakes:	minus mistakes:	minus mistakes:
equals cwpm:	equals cwpm:	equals cwpm:

Passage 87: Excerpt From: *The Old Curiosity Shop* by Charles Dickens

Although I am an old man, night is generally my time for walking. In the	16
summer I often leave home early in the morning, and roam about fields and lanes	31
all day, or even escape for days or weeks together; but, saving in the country, I	47
seldom go out until after dark, though, Heaven be thanked, I love its light and	62
feel the cheerfulness it sheds upon the earth, as much as any creature living.	76
I have fallen insensibly into this habit, both because it favors my infirmity and	90
because it affords me greater opportunity of speculating on the characters and	102
occupations of those who fill the streets. The glare and hurry of broad noon are	117
not adapted to idle pursuits like mine; a glimpse of passing faces caught by the	132
light of a street-lamp or a shop window is often better for my purpose than their	148
full revelation in the daylight; and, if I must add the truth, night is kinder in this	165
respect than day, which too often destroys an air-built castle at the moment of its	181
completion, without the least ceremony or remorse.	188
That constant pacing to and fro, that never-ending restlessness, that incessant	200
tread of feet wearing the rough stones smooth and glossy—is it not a wonder how	216
the dwellers in narrows ways can bear to hear it! Think of a sick man in such a	234
place as Saint Martin's Court, listening to the footsteps, and in the midst of pain	249
and weariness obliged, despite himself (as though it were a task he must	262
perform) to detect the child's step from the man's, the slipshod beggar from the	276
booted exquisite, the lounging from the busy, the dull heel of the sauntering	289
outcast from the quick tread of an expectant pleasure-seeker—think of the hum	303
and noise always being present to his sense, and of the stream of life that will not	320
stop, pouring on, on, on, through all his restless dreams, as if he were condemned	335
to lie, dead but conscious, in a noisy churchyard, and had no hope of rest for	351
centuries to come.	354

Words Read:	Words Read:	Words Read:
minus mistakes:	minus mistakes:	minus mistakes:
equals cwpm:	equals cwpm:	equals cwpm:

Passage 88: Excerpt From: Chapter 2 of *Moby Dick*

I stuffed a shirt or two into my old carpet-bag, tucked it under my arm, and	17
started for Cape Horn and the Pacific. Quitting the good city of old Manhatto, I	32
duly arrived in New Bedford. It was a Saturday night in December. Much was I	47
disappointed upon learning that the little packet for Nantucket had already	58
sailed, and that no way of reaching that place would offer, till the following	72
Monday.	73
As most young candidates for the pains and penalties of whaling stop at this	87
same New Bedford, thence to embark on their voyage, it may as well be related	102
that I, for one, had no idea of so doing. For my mind was made up to sail in no	122
other than a Nantucket craft, because there was a fine, boisterous something	134
about everything connected with that famous old island, which amazingly	144
pleased me. Besides though New Bedford has of late been gradually	155
monopolizing the business of whaling, and though in this matter poor old	167
Nantucket is now much behind her, yet Nantucket was her great original—the	180
place where the first dead American whale was stranded. Where else but from	193
Nantucket did those aboriginal whalemen, the Red-Men, first sally out in canoes	206
to give chase to the Leviathan? And where but from Nantucket, too, did that first	221
adventurous little sloop put forth, partly laden with imported cobblestones—so	232
goes the story—to throw at the whales, in order to discover when they were nigh	248
enough to risk a harpoon from the bowsprit?	256
Now having a night, a day, and still another night following before me in New	271
Bedford, ere I could embark for my destined port, it became a matter of	285
concernment where I was to eat and sleep meanwhile. It was a very dubious-	299
looking, nay, a very dark and dismal night, bitingly cold and cheerless. I knew no	317
one in the place.	321

Words Read:	Words Read:	Words Read:
minus mistakes:	minus mistakes:	minus mistakes:
equals cwpm:	equals cwpm:	equals cwpm:

Name: _____

Passage 89: Cinderella Tech - Part 1

Once upon a startup pitch, in a bustling city where skyscrapers glistened and | 13
Wi-Fi was as abundant as coffee shops, there lived a young, ingenious coder | 26
named Ella, known in the tech world as "Cinder." Why "Cinder"? Well, that's a tale | 40
as old as innovation itself. | 45

Cinder was raised by her not-so-wicked but slightly insufferable stepmother, | 57
Deborah, an investment banker with an eye for profit and a nose for insider | 71
trading. Deborah had two daughters of her own, Divina and Esmerelda, who were | 84
social media influencers obsessed with perfect selfies, viral trends, and | 94
"networking" at every tech party in town. Cinder, however, had different dreams. | 96
While her stepsisters plastered filters over their faces, she was deep in her garage | 110
workshop, tinkering with circuit boards, coding late into the night, and dreaming | 222
of launching the tech world's next unicorn. | 229

Now, Ella didn't mind her family too much—well, except for their endless | 242
comments about how "real entrepreneurs don't wear hoodies and messy buns." | 253
They failed to see her vision, dismissing her AI-powered app, "Fit It," which could | 268
instantly assemble a perfect outfit from one's wardrobe using the magic of | 280
machine learning and a tiny sprinkle of Cinder's signature coding wizardry. | 291

But it was hard to run a budding startup with Divina and Esmerelda around. | 305
They'd "borrow" her gadgets for selfies and delete her code to free up storage for | 320
their photo archives. Worst of all, her stepmother declared that all Cinder's profits | 333
would go to "household expenses" if she ever made it big. Cinder was always left | 248
to do the "menial work"—troubleshooting, debugging, and maintaining the | 257
family's technology. It was a life of silent grinding and quiet code. | 269

Words Read:	Words Read:	Words Read:
minus mistakes:	minus mistakes:	minus mistakes:
equals cwpm:	equals cwpm:	equals cwpm:

104

Passage 90: Cinderella Tech - Part 2

One day, news buzzed across every startup hub in town: Prince, the tech | 13
industry's most enigmatic VC, was throwing an exclusive Tech Gala. The rumor | 25
was, he was looking to fund one groundbreaking new startup, with a million- | 38
dollar investment on the spot. Only the best minds in tech were invited, and | 52
Cinder knew her app could blow the others out of the water. She just had to find a | 70
way to get in. | 74

"Oh, please, *you*?" scoffed Divina. "Prince wants influencers and geniuses, not | 85
garage-dwelling geeks who can barely keep their cloud storage organized." | 96

Esmerelda piled on. "Besides, you wouldn't have anything to wear." | 106

Cinder tried to ignore them, but she felt a pang. She didn't care about clothes, | 121
but she needed that chance to pitch her product, to prove herself. She returned to | 136
her workshop feeling defeated but determined. | 142

As she slumped over her laptop, she heard a ping—a Gmail notification. She | 156
opened the email, and there it was: a message from a mysterious sender called | 170
"FayeGodma Tech Solutions Inc." | 174

"You've got potential, kid. Check the downloads folder." | 182

Curious, Cinder checked. There sat a fully-customizable holographic invitation | 192
to the Tech Gala, along with a freshly coded wardrobe app that could instantly | 206
project any outfit onto her. She clicked through the app, and her screen displayed | 220
the perfect startup chic look: a sleek, stylish, eco-friendly jumpsuit that looked | 233
straight out of a futuristic fashion mag. Cinder beamed. | 242

"Oh, and don't worry about transportation," FayeGodma messaged in another | 252
email. "Check the driveway at 7:00 sharp." | 259

At exactly 7:00, she peeked outside. There, gleaming under the garage lights, | 271
was a self-driving Tesla, shimmering in a metallic, fairy-dust silver. | 283

"Midnight return policy," said the Tesla's digital voice assistant as she climbed | 295
in. "All temporary code will vanish. Don't lose track of time, Ms. Cinder." | 308

Words Read:	Words Read:	Words Read:
minus mistakes:	minus mistakes:	minus mistakes:
equals cwpm:	equals cwpm:	equals cwpm:

Passage 91: Cinderella Tech - Part 3

Cinder arrived at the Gala, feeling more powerful than ever in her holographic	13
outfit. The stepsisters were there, chattering endlessly to various investors, but	24
they didn't recognize her with her polished look and confident grin.	35
Then, the room fell silent as he appeared: Prince, the venture capitalist of every	49
startup's dreams. He was tall, mysterious, with a smartwatch that cost more than	62
a year's rent, and a reputation for investing in companies that changed the world.	76
One by one, entrepreneurs took the stage, pitching their projects. Finally, it was	89
Cinder's turn.	91
She stepped up and pulled up her app, which projected her pitch in an	105
augmented reality format. With each swipe, "Fit It" demonstrated its ability to	116
scan wardrobes, offer sustainable fashion choices, and eliminate the need for	127
wasteful shopping. The audience gasped in awe, and Prince's eyebrows raised—a	139
clear sign of interest.	143
"Impressive," he said, his voice smooth as a premium Bluetooth speaker. "And	155
you're the sole developer?"	159
"Yes," Cinder said, her voice unwavering. "It's my design, my code. I've built it	173
from the ground up."	177
Prince was about to ask more, but then—ping! The Tesla's voice assistant	190
chimed into her earpiece. "Eleven fifty-five, Ms. Cinder. Recommend wrapping it	202
up."	203
In a moment of sheer panic, she thanked the crowd, dropped her contact info	217
with Prince, and dashed out of the Gala. But in her hurry, she left behind a single	234
USB drive containing her code—a backup she'd made in case of a system failure.	249
The next day, the tech world was abuzz. Prince was on a mission to find the	265
owner of the mysterious USB drive. The media spun endless stories about the	278
"mystery coder." Divina and Esmerelda claimed they were the mysterious	288
"Cinder," but failed to show a single line of code that could match her innovation.	303

Words Read:	Words Read:	Words Read:
minus mistakes:	minus mistakes:	minus mistakes:
equals cwpm:	equals cwpm:	equals cwpm:

Name: _____

Passage 92: Cinderella Tech - Part 4

Meanwhile, Cinder was back in her garage, furiously coding, hoping she hadn't | 12
blown her one shot. Then came a knock at the door. She opened it to find Prince, | 29
holding the USB drive. | 33

"I believe this is yours?" he said, smirking. | 41

Cinder gulped. "I thought you'd just fund another app by now. You really came | 55
all this way?" | 58

"Talent like yours doesn't come around often," he replied. "And besides, I need | 71
the person who made this. No one else could." | 80

With a grin, Cinder took the USB drive, plugged it into her laptop, and showed | 95
him her latest update. Prince was floored and offered her the million-dollar | 108
investment on the spot. | 112

With Prince's backing, "Fit It" grew into a powerhouse in sustainable fashion | 124
tech. Cinder's app was a hit, and soon, she was a tech mogul herself, complete | 139
with her own electric car fleet and a wardrobe far beyond her days of hand-me- | 155
downs. Deborah, Divina, and Esmerelda tried to cozy up to her newfound success, | 168
but she simply offered them a lifetime subscription to her app and suggested | 181
they find their own "happily ever after." | 188

And so, Cinder went from garage geek to girl boss, proving that with the right | 203
mix of talent, tech, and maybe a little fairy-code-mother magic, anyone can | 217
rewrite their own fairytale. | 221

The moral of this modern Cinderella story is: **Believe in your own vision,** | 234
embrace your unique skills, and don't let anyone else's expectations hold you | 246
back. True success doesn't come from fitting in—it comes from innovating, | 258
standing out, and daring to take the leap. | 266

Or, in startup lingo: *Stay true to your code, keep debugging your dreams, and* | 280
remember: every unicorn begins in a garage. | 287

Even when the odds seem stacked against you, perseverance, creativity, and | 298
a touch of unexpected support can turn your vision into reality. | 309

Words Read:	Words Read:	Words Read:
minus mistakes:	minus mistakes:	minus mistakes:
equals cwpm:	equals cwpm:	equals cwpm:

Passage 93: Rapunzel and the Green Gear – Part 1

Once upon a time, in a kingdom that faced both wolf troubles and worsening	14
weather patterns, there lived an inventor named Rapunzel. Now, Rapunzel wasn't	25
your typical tower-bound princess. Sure, she lived in a tall tower—her foster	39
mother, a local botanist, had built it to give Rapunzel a stunning view of the	54
kingdom's forests, which were being devoured by the dreaded Big Bad Wolf and	67
his loyal pack. But Rapunzel wasn't one to just stare out the window and sigh.	82
From her vantage point, she noticed an alarming trend: the forests were	94
thinning, the rivers were drying, and the air was thick with smoke from wildfires	108
set by the wolf to drive humans out of "his territory." Rapunzel knew that if things	124
didn't change, the land would become uninhabitable—for wolves, humans, and	135
everything in between. So she got to work.	143
In her tower, Rapunzel tinkered day and night, studying everything from wind	155
currents to carbon cycles to lupine psychology. Finally, after many nights of	167
inventing (and one accidental tower fire), she completed her masterpiece: the	178
Green Gear, an eco-technology wonder. This sleek, portable device could convert	190
smoke into clean air, plant seeds faster than you could say "bibbidi-bobbidi-boo,"	204
and even sprinkle "wolf-safe" repellant to protect the freshly planted trees. It was	218
solar-powered, naturally, and came with a satellite to track wolf movement and	231
monitor the climate's health.	235
One day, Rapunzel heard the howls of the Big Bad Wolf approaching the edge	249
of her tower's forest. With a determined smile, she grabbed the Green Gear, tied	263
her long braids into a practical bun, and rappelled down the tower wall like an	278
eco-warrior on a mission.	283
As she stepped into the clearing, the Big Bad Wolf emerged from the shadows,	297
all fangs and fur, his golden eyes gleaming with menace. "Well, well, what do we	312
have here?" he sneered. "Another human thinking she can boss around the	324
forest?"	325

Words Read:	Words Read:	Words Read:
minus mistakes:	minus mistakes:	minus mistakes:
equals cwpm:	equals cwpm:	equals cwpm:

Passage 94: Rapunzel and the Green Gear – Part 2

As she stepped into the clearing, the Big Bad Wolf emerged from the shadows,	14
all fangs and fur, his golden eyes gleaming with menace. "Well, well, what do we	29
have here?" he sneered. "Another human thinking she can boss around the	41
forest?"	42
Rapunzel didn't flinch. "Not bossing, just balancing. You're turning this forest	53
into a wasteland, and I've had enough."	60
"Oh, I'm just a wolf trying to make a living," he growled. "People build houses	75
where my pack roams, set fires, hunt our prey…so now I take back what's mine.	91
Scorched earth!"	93
"Well, you're not the only one with a plan," Rapunzel said, clicking a button on	108
her Green Gear. With a hum and a flash, the device sent out a cloud of tiny seeds	126
across the clearing. Saplings began to sprout almost immediately, roots weaving	137
into the ground and leaves stretching toward the sky.	146
The wolf's eyes widened. "What…is that?"	153
Rapunzel grinned. "Instant reforestation. And that's not all." She turned a dial,	165
and the device emitted a deep, resonating sound that pulsed through the	177
clearing. The wolf took a step back, wincing.	185
"What is that horrible noise?" he growled, his fur bristling.	195
"A frequency that only wolves can hear. A bit annoying, isn't it? But the more	210
you threaten the balance here, the louder it'll get. If you cooperate, it'll stay	224
silent."	225
The wolf narrowed his eyes. "You're bluffing."	232
"Am I?" Rapunzel turned up the frequency just a tad, and the wolf yelped,	246
covering his ears. Then she pressed another button, and a gust of cool, purified	260
air whooshed through the clearing, blowing away the smoke from the last fire	273
he'd set. "See, Big Bad, I'm not your enemy. But if you keep tearing down the	289
forest, I'll make this place very unpleasant for you."	298

Words Read:	Words Read:	Words Read:
minus mistakes:	minus mistakes:	minus mistakes:
equals cwpm:	equals cwpm:	equals cwpm:

Name: _____

Passage 95: Rapunzel and the Green Gear – Part 3

"Am I?" Rapunzel turned up the frequency just a tad, and the wolf yelped, | 14
covering his ears. Then she pressed another button, and a gust of cool, purified | 28
air whooshed through the clearing, blowing away the smoke from the last fire | 41
he'd set. "See, Big Bad, I'm not your enemy. But if you keep tearing down the | 57
forest, I'll make this place very unpleasant for you." | 66

The Big Bad Wolf glared at her, but he knew when he was beat. "Fine," he | 82
growled, lowering his ears and grumbling under his breath. "But my pack and I | 96
need space. Food. I want a peace treaty." | 104

Rapunzel raised an eyebrow. "How about a green treaty instead? You and your | 117
pack can have your space—but no more fires. We'll work out a grazing rotation | 132
and install some of these eco-sensors to make sure the forests stay intact for | 147
both wolves and people." | 151

The wolf considered her offer. He wasn't happy, but he wasn't foolish either. | 164
"Deal," he muttered. | 167

And with a handshake (well, paw-shake) that echoed through the forest, | 179
Rapunzel and the Big Bad Wolf struck an agreement that marked the beginning | 192
of a new era in the kingdom. Rapunzel used her Green Gear to restore the land, | 208
and the wolf's pack kept the deer population in check, preventing overgrazing. | 220
The forest flourished, the air grew clear, and Rapunzel became a legendary | 232
figure—not for her hair, but for her brain and bravery. | 243

The Big Bad Wolf? Well, he became a legendary conservationist too, guarding | 255
the balance in the woods. And whenever he felt like a bit of mischief, Rapunzel | 270
just had to reach for the volume on her Green Gear, and he'd scamper away with | 296
his tail between his legs. | 291

Words Read:	Words Read:	Words Read:
minus mistakes:	minus mistakes:	minus mistakes:
equals cwpm:	equals cwpm:	equals cwpm:

Passage 96: Aurora Bright – Part 1

Once upon a high-rise in the bustling heart of Silicon City, there was a savvy	16
and brilliant CEO named Aurora Bright. Aurora was the founder of SleepTech, a	29
groundbreaking tech company specializing in innovative wellness apps designed	38
to help people get the perfect night's sleep. With a head for business and a heart	54
for betterment, Aurora took her company to incredible heights. But, as fairy tales	67
(and the business world) go, she had a few… complications.	77
Aurora had been warned at the very start of her career by her fairy god-	92
mentors, a group of veteran businesswomen with titles like "Chief Enchantment	103
Officer" and "Vibe Coordinator," about the cutthroat world of business. "Beware	114
of burnout," the fairies said in hushed whispers over oat milk lattes. "Pace	127
yourself, or you'll fall into the dreaded sleep slump."	136
However, Aurora was unstoppable. Fueled by green juice and the dream of	148
SleepTech's IPO, she worked tirelessly. But little did she know that one of her	162
board members, a rather cantankerous woman named Mal Volent, had a	173
vendetta against her. Mal was the kind of executive who loved buzzwords like	186
"synergy" and "disruption" but was always more interested in scheming than	197
strategy. She thought Aurora was far too idealistic for the "sleep industry." Her	210
world domination plans involved setting people up with insomnia and then	221
making them pay for the cure—a philosophy Aurora wholeheartedly rejected.	232
Mal concocted a plan to bring Aurora down. She created a cursed "innovation"	245
she called the Prickly Pitch Deck, full of graphs with misleading projections,	257
endless slides of fine print, and bar charts with dizzying colors. At a critical	271
investor meeting, Mal slipped the Prickly Pitch Deck into Aurora's presentation.	282

Words Read:	Words Read:	Words Read:
minus mistakes:	minus mistakes:	minus mistakes:
equals cwpm:	equals cwpm:	equals cwpm:

Passage 97: Aurora Bright – Part 2

Aurora, running on three espressos and four hours of sleep, opened the cursed	13
deck, and at the sight of the terrible, overwhelming presentation, she felt the	26
exhaustion slam into her like a freight train. She yawned, then yawned again, and	40
before she knew it, she was slumped over her laptop, deeply asleep.	52

But this wasn't just any nap; it was the Big Burnout. Rumors flew that she would 68
sleep for a hundred years or until a well-rested executive with a heart of gold 84
would come and help her out of her work slump. Her fairies tried everything from 99
offkey singing to loud alarm clocks, but nothing could wake Aurora. 110

For the next few quarters, SleepTech floundered. It was taken over by Mal 123
Volent, who rebranded it as "NoRest Industries" and pushed products like "Sleep 134
Debt Solutions" and "Premium Power Naps." The company's stock took a 145
nosedive, and soon, Mal found herself in financial hot water, with investors pulling 158
out left and right. 162

But hope was not lost. Enter Phillip Hart, a young CEO from a social impact 177
company called HeartBeats. Phillip had always admired Aurora's work, and when 188
he heard of her Big Burnout, he was determined to revive her spirit and restore 203
SleepTech to its original mission. Phillip wasn't your average executive; he 214
believed in work-life balance, the power of wellness, and the impact of good 228
sleep. 229

He arrived at SleepTech with an inspiring vision board, a PowerPoint deck of 242
heart-centered innovations, and a strong supply of strong tea. He sat beside 255
Aurora, gently telling her about his own journey and reading the last quarter's 268
uplifting stock reports (which he'd improved by purchasing massive shares of 279
SleepTech stock, much to Mal Volent's chagrin). Inspired by his sincerity and the 292
aroma of revitalizing strong tea, Aurora stirred. 299

Words Read:	Words Read:	Words Read:
minus mistakes:	minus mistakes:	minus mistakes:
equals cwpm:	equals cwpm:	equals cwpm:

Passage 98: Aurora Bright – Part 3

He arrived at SleepTech with an inspiring vision board, a PowerPoint deck of	13
heart-centered innovations, and a strong supply of strong tea. He sat beside	26
Aurora, gently telling her about his own journey and reading the last quarter's	39
uplifting stock reports (which he'd improved by purchasing massive shares of	50
SleepTech stock, much to Mal Volent's chagrin). Inspired by his sincerity and the	63
aroma of revitalizing strong tea, Aurora stirred.	70

Finally, with a gentle yawn and a blinking of eyes, she sat up straight in her ergonomic chair. "Who are you?" she asked, sleepily but with a gleam of ambition in her eyes.

"Just a fellow CEO who believes in a dream," Phillip replied, offering her a freshly brewed, herbal-infused "Rise and Shine" tea.

Aurora felt her energy return, and with it, her determination. Together, she and Phillip orchestrated a hostile takeover to oust Mal Volent from her ill-gotten position. They revamped SleepTech, bringing it back to its original vision of wellness, and even launched a line of sustainable "Work-Life Harmony" products that became an instant hit.

Aurora went on to inspire other executives with her story of burnout and revival, advocating for workplace wellness and healthy boundaries. Her company became the gold standard of corporate culture, and she and Phillip teamed up as co-CEOs, making the perfect balance between dreamers and doers.

And they lived… well, they worked happily ever after, at a steady pace with plenty of vacation days and a mandatory nap room for all employees.

Line count	
	86
	100
	103
	117
	125
	138
	151
	163
	175
	180
	193
	203
	214
	224
	238
	250

Words Read:	Words Read:	Words Read:
minus mistakes:	minus mistakes:	minus mistakes:
equals cwpm:	equals cwpm:	equals cwpm:

Passage 99: Alice in the Cyber-Wood – Part 1

Once upon a time, in a world woven with wires and wonder, there lived a   15

curious girl named Alice, always armed with her augmented reality glasses. One   27

day, she received a message on her holographic watch from her Grandma. "Bring   40

me some bandwidth biscuits and virtual veggie stew," it read. Grandma was tech-   53

savvy and slightly eccentric, living in a cabin camouflaged in the depths of the   67

Cyber-Wood.   69

Alice, always up for an adventure, donned her crimson-coded cloak (a gift from   83

her Grandma that boasted both style and stealth mode) and set out on her   97

electric scooter. As she zipped along the digital dales, she veered off the well-   111

worn road, drawn by a glitching graphic—a white-hat hacker in a waistcoat,   125

muttering about being late for a server meeting.   133

"Follow me to the deepest directory!" the rabbit-like rogue beckoned, his voice   146

crackling like static. Curiosity was high. Alice couldn't resist. She pressed a button   159

on her cloak, activating its "Follow-the-Figure" function, and soon found herself   172

spiraling down a fiber-optic funnel into a strange, simulated world known as   185

Wonder-Web.   187

In this curious cyber-space, code cascaded like candy-colored confetti, and   199

binary butterflies fluttered above her head. Alice's first stop was at a pixelated   212

picnic, hosted by a half-mad Machine Learning Mad Hatter and a perpetually   225

debugging Dormouse.   227

"Tea or VR?" the Mad Hatter asked, tipping his USB-brimmed hat. "Or perhaps   241

a touch of toast with terabyte topping?"   248

Alice opted for the VR goggles and suddenly found herself in a swirling, surreal   262

tea party—complete with digital donuts that dissolved into data upon tasting. But   275

the immersive experience was soon interrupted by a popup warning: 285

Approaching malware detected.   288

As Alice peeled off her goggles, she spotted the notorious Big Bad Data Wolf   302

lurking nearby, his data-dripping jaws gnashing.   309

Words Read:	Words Read:	Words Read:
minus mistakes:	minus mistakes:	minus mistakes:
equals cwpm:	equals cwpm:	equals cwpm:

Passage 100: Alice in the Cyber-Wood – Part 2

"Heading to Grandma's, are we?" he growled, his voice smooth as synthetic | 12

silk. "Why not share the shortcut protocol? I promise I'll patch things up with her," | 27

he said, his smirk a sneaky subroutine of deceit. | 36

Alice was no noob, though. She smiled sweetly and activated her voice | 48

assistant, RedBot. "Track the Wolf's IP address and set a silent alarm to notify | 62

Grandma's security system," she whispered. | 67

But the wolf, with his eyes aglow in LED yellow, was already sprinting through | 81

the Cyber-Wood. When she arrived at Grandma's she found the door ajar—a sure | 96

sign of system breach. Inside, the wolf had shape-shifted into Grandma's avatar. | 109

"What bug-eyed specs you have!" Alice remarked, sarcastically. | 118

"All the better to spot your software with, my dear," replied the wolf, trying | 132

hard to mask his true voice under Grandma's soothing Siri-like tone. | 144

"And what gigantic gadgets you have!" she added, inching closer. | 154

"All the better to scan your data with!" the wolf roared, lunging forward. But | 168

Alice was ready. With a swipe of her smartwatch, she deployed a firewall flare | 182

that sent the wolf howling back, his pixels scattering into harmless bits of binary. | 196

Grandma, who had been safely spectating from her secure cloud server, | 207

quickly teleported back into her smart home. "Thank goodness for two-factor | 219

authentication!" she exclaimed, giving Alice a holographic hug. | 227

The duo then settled down for a cozy evening of cookies coded with care and a | 243

game of virtual reality chess. As the Cyber-Wood settled into its nighttime mode, | 257

with its neon trees dimming and circuits humming softly, Alice smiled. She had | 270

learned a valuable lesson that day: curiosity may lead you down complex code | 283

paths, but cleverness keeps you from crashing. | 290

And so, in the glow of Grandma's high-tech hearth, Alice and her grandmother | 304

laughed and toasted to triumph over technology—a tale of wits, wires, and | 317

wonder in a world where the lines between the digital and the dreamlike had | 331

delightfully blurred. | 333

Words Read:	Words Read:	Words Read:
minus mistakes:	minus mistakes:	minus mistakes:
equals cwpm:	equals cwpm:	equals cwpm:

Frequency _____

					5
					10
					15
					20
					25
					20
					35
					40
					45
					50
					55
					60
					65
					70
					75
					80
					85
					90
					95
					100

Words Read: _____
minus mistakes: _____
equals cwpm: _____

Words Read: _____
minus mistakes: _____
equals cwpm: _____

Words Read: _____
minus mistakes: _____
equals cwpm: _____

Fluency Tracking

Name: _____ Period: _____

Passage #	Date	CWPM	Date	CWPM	Date	CWPM	Date	CWPM

Each of the passages, comprehension pages can be scored on the attached rubric; however, if you would like sample answers for each passage in the form of the **Answer Key** you see on this page, please email: twopencilsandabook@gmail.com and we'll send it to you.

Name: _____

Fluency Passage: _Serena Williams_____

Directions: Use Complete sentences to answer the following questions:

After First Read:

Summary (four sentences):
Serena Williams is considered one of the greatest athletes of all time, holding 23 Grand Slam singles titles and ranking world No. 1 for 319 weeks. She achieved the rare "Serena Slam" by winning all four Grand Slam singles titles consecutively from 2002 to 2003. Serena has also excelled in earnings, consistently ranking among the top-paid athletes, both male and female. Besides tennis, she has numerous brand endorsements and holds a minority ownership in the Miami Dolphins alongside her sister, Venus.

After Second Read:

Central Idea:
The central idea of the reading is that Serena Williams has achieved unparalleled success and influence in the world of sports, especially as a female athlete.

Best Evidence Supporting the Central Idea:
"She has won 23 Grand Slam singles titles, the most by any player in the Open Era, and the second-most of all time."
This quote illustrates Serena's record-breaking achievements, emphasizing her success in a highly competitive sport.

How the Central Idea Is Developed:
The central idea is developed by highlighting Serena's record-breaking accomplishments in tennis, her financial success as one of the highest-paid athletes, and her endorsements with major brands. Her achievements in both tennis and business demonstrate her influence and significance as an athlete. Additionally, her role as a minority owner in a major sports team further illustrates her wide-ranging impact.

After Third Read

Inference Paragraph:
Based on the information in the passage, one can infer that Serena Williams' success has had a substantial impact on the perception of women in sports and their earning potential. Although historically male athletes have earned more and received more endorsements, Serena has broken through these barriers, consistently ranking among the top-paid athletes in the world. Her ability to secure high-profile endorsements and ranking among the top 100 highest-paid athletes highlights her influence. This not only showcases her individual talent but also signals a shift in how female athletes are valued and can inspire future generations to pursue sports professionally.

25

Research

Abbott, M., Wills, H., Miller, A., & Kaufman, J. (2012). The relationship of error rate and comprehension in second and third grade oral reading fluency. Reading Psychology, 33(1–2), 104–132.

Chard, D. J., Vaughn, S., & Tyler, B. J. (2002). A synthesis of research on effective interventions for building reading fluency with elementary students with learning disabilities. Journal of Learning Disabilities, 35(5), 386–406.

Chomsky, C. (1976). After decoding: What? Language Arts, 53(3), 288–296.

Deno, S. L., Mirkin, P. K., & Chiang, B. (1982). Identifying valid measures of reading. Exceptional Children, 49, 36-43.

Deno, S. (2003). Developments in curriculum-based measurement. The Journal of Special Education, 37, 184-192. doi:10.1177/00224669030370030801 http://digitalcommons.unl.edu/buroscurriculum/3.

Eldredge, J. L., & Quinn, D. W. (1988). Increasing reading performance of low-achieving second graders with dyad reading groups. Journal of Educational Research, 82(1), 40–46.

Fuchs, L. S., Fuchs, D., Hamlett, C. L., Walz, L., & Germann, G. (1993). Formative evaluation of academic progress: How much growth can we expect? School Psychology Review, 22(1), 27–48.

Fuchs, L. S., Fuchs, D., Hamlett, C. L., & Whinnery, K. (1991). Effects of goal line feedback on level, slope, and stability of performance within curriculum-based measurement. Learning Disabilities Research and Practice, 6(2), 66–74.

Fuchs, L. S., Fuchs, D., Hosp, M. K., & Jenkins, J. R. (2001). Oral reading fluency as an indicator of reading competence: A theoretical, empirical, and historical analysis. Scientific Studies of Reading, 5(3), 239–256.

Hasbrouck, J., & Tindal, G (2005). Oral reading fluency: 90 years of measurement (Tech. Rep. No. 33, Behavioral Research and Teaching (BRT)). University of Oregon, College of Education.

Hasbrouck, J., & Tindal, G. A. (2006). Oral reading fluency norms: A valuable assessment tool for reading teachers. The Reading Teacher. 59(7),636–644.

Hasbrouck, J., & Tindal, G. (2017). An update to the compiled ORF norms (Technical Report No. 1702). Eugene, OR: Behavioral Research and Teaching, University of Oregon.

Heckelman, R. G. (1969). A neurological-impress method of remedial-reading instruction. Academic Therapy Quarterly, 5(4), 277–282.

Klauda, S. L., & Guthrie, J. T. (2008). Relationships of three components of reading fluency to reading comprehension. Journal of Educational Psychology, 100(2), 310–321.

Kim, Y., Petscher, Y., Schatschneider, C., & Foorman, B. (2010). Does growth rate in oral reading fluency matter in predicting reading comprehension achievement? Journal of Educational Psychology, 102(3), 652–667.

Kuhn, M. R., Schwanenflugel, P. J., & Meisinger, E. B. (2010). Aligning theory and assessment of reading fluency: Automaticity, prosody, and definitions of fluency. Reading Research Quarterly, 45(2), 230–251.

Kuhn, M. R., & Stahl, S. A. (2003). Fluency: A review of developmental and remedial practices. Journal of Educational Psychology, 95(1), 3–21.

LaBerge, D., & Samuels, S. J. (1974). Toward a theory of automatic information processing in reading. Cognitive Psychology, 6(2), 292–323.

Lee, J., & Yoon Yoon, S. (2015). The effects of repeated reading on reading fluency for students with reading disabilities: A meta-analysis. Journal of Learning Disabilities, 50(2), 213–224.

Morgan, P. L., & Sideridis, G. D. (2006). Contrasting the effectiveness of fluency interventions for students with or at risk for learning disabilities: A multilevel random coefficient modeling metaanalysis. Learning Disabilities Research & Practice, 21(4), 191–210.

Morgan, P. L., Sideridis, G., & Hua, Y. (2011). Initial and over-time effects of fluency interventions for students with or at risk for disabilities. The Journal of Special Education, 46(2), 94–116.

National Institute of Child Health and Human Development. (2000a). Report of the National Reading Panel. Teaching children to read: An evidence-based assessment of the scientific research literature on reading and its implications for reading instruction (NIH Publication No. 00-4769). Washington, DC: U.S. Government Printing Office.

National Institute of Child Health and Human Development. (2000b). Report of the National Reading Panel. Teaching children to read: An evidence-based assessment of the scientific research literature on reading and its implications for reading instruction: Reports of the subgroups (NIH Publication No. 00-4754). Washington, DC: U.S. Government Printing Office.

Price, K. W., Meisinger, E. B., Louwerse, M. M., & D'Mello, S. (2015). The contributions of oral and silent reading fluency to reading comprehension. Reading Psychology, 37(2), 167–201.

Prior, S. M., Fenwick, K. D., Saunders, K.S., Ouellette, R., O'Quinn, C., & Harney, S. (2011). Comprehension after oral and silent reading: Does grade level matter? Literacy Research and Instruction, 50(3), 183–194.

Reutzel, D. R., & Hollingsworth, P. M. (1993). Effects of fluency training on second graders' reading comprehension. Journal of Educational Research, 86(6), 325–331.

Schwanenflugel, P. J., Meisinger, E. B., Wisenbaker, J. M., Kuhn, M. R., Strauss, G. P., Morris, R. D. (2006). Becoming a fluent and automatic reader in the early elementary school years. Reading Research Quarterly, 41(4), 496–522.

Therrien, W. J. (2004). Fluency and comprehension gains as a result of repeated reading. Remedial and Special Education, 25(4), 252–261.

Williamson, G.L. (2004). Student readiness for postsecondary options. Durham, NC: MetaMetrics.

Williamson, G.L. (2008). A text readability continuum for postsecondary readiness. Journal of Advanced Academics, 19 (4), 602-632.

Sign-up for Two Pencils and a Book Newsletter for classroom tips, freebies, extra passages monthly and an immediate freebie that includes 30 additional fiction fluency passages – each written at two levels.

Email: twopencilsandabook@gmail.com – put 134 High School Fluency in the body of the email.

Check Out These Additional Titles

Phonics Fluency for Older Struggling Readers:
https://www.amazon.com/dp/B0D4JCVKSV

Science of Reading Decodable Reader 2 Phonics for Older Struggling Readers: Decodable Reader 2
https://www.amazon.com/dp/B0DCW2GYMV

High Interest Low Level Reading Comprehension and Fluency - Popular Amusement Park Rides
https://www.amazon.com/dp/B0CVNN19Y6

Frankenstein Adapted Novel Science of Reading Unit in High Interest Low Level Passages with EDI, Reading Comprehension, Fluency and More: Frankenstein ... Novel Unit (Adapted Novels and Novel Units)
https://www.amazon.com/dp/B0DDTFXR8V

Made in United States
North Haven, CT
26 December 2024

63543070R00070